THE BEACH TOWNS

LIBRARY OF CONGRESS CATALOGING IN PUBLICATION DATA

Pierson, Robert John.

  The beach towns.

  Includes index.
  1. Los Angeles (Calif.)—Description—Guide-books.
  2. Walking—California—Los Angeles—Guide-books.
  3. Beaches—California—Los Angeles—Guide-books.
I. Title.
F869.L83P54 1985 917.94'930946 84-19912
ISBN 0-87701-312-8 (pbk.)

EDITING
Kate Edgar

BOOK AND COVER DESIGN
Linda Herman

TYPOGRAPHY
Accent & Alphabet

Chronicle Books
One Hallidie Plaza
San Francisco, CA 94102

THE BEACH TOWNS

A Walker's Guide
to L.A.'s Beach Communities

by Robert John Pierson

Chronicle Books • San Francisco

ACKNOWLEDGMENTS

I don't know if there is a way *not* to make an acknowledgment section sound like an Academy Award acceptance speech, but here goes. . . .

This guidebook represents hundreds of hours of avid citywalking. Perhaps the people who challenged and informed me most concerning the life of city streets and urban villages were a few professors and instructors. Special appreciation must be expressed to Rusty Springer, Don Miller, Christopher Salter, Carol Warren, Ray Anderson, and Jim Keith.

I want to say a special thank you to each of my friends, who have supported and encouraged this project, as well as put up with continual bursts of "walk talk." Sincere gratitude particularly to Craig Hendrickson, Elaine Lyford, Tom Wilcox, John Berger, Holly Barlow, Dave Crane, Steve Preston, Lena Kasarjian, Dallas and Jane Williard, Richard Natali, Donna and John Countess-Lackey, and Michael Hoopes. And to Bob Blomeley, who encouraged me and believed in my work when times were really tough. And to my Dad and Judy.

Also, I'd like to express appreciation to a few remarkable people who love L.A.: Dan Hoye, Rita Lynch, and Deborah Perrin.

One other very important group in this endeavor were the countless villagers in the coastal communities who opened their homes, cafes, and shops to share their special love and affection for their villages. Without their generous enthusiasm and information, this guidebook would be just another tourist's diary.

Finally, thanks to my lawyer Roger Horwitz and my editor Kate Edgar, both of whom provided beacons of assurance and insight in the finer details of this new venture.

Blessings on you all.

CONTENTS

PREFACE

A walking guide to L.A.? For many people, Los Angeles and citywalking are contradictions. As the song goes, "Nobody walks in L.A."

In fact, no other American city has been as overlooked, misunderstood, and stereotyped by urban walkers. Viewed as the epitome of the modern car-crazed megalopolis, the Big Orange is ridiculed by many as all peel and no substance.

Yet L.A. is more than just a city. Encompassing nearly five hundred miles, ranging from sandy beaches and deep canyons to broad valleys and steep mountains, extending into a wider urban region of over twelve million people representing every race, religion, culture, and lifestyle, Los Angeles is a richly complex network of hundreds of vibrant villages, many of which are unique, exciting places for citywalking.

L.A. is a frustratingly difficult city to know and understand. Its complexity and enormity often overwhelm residents and visitors alike. With its tangles of freeways, often the only images many people have of Los Angeles are blurs from the car window and quick visits to snappy tourist attractions. But more and more people want to experience a richer understanding of Los Angeles as a city of villages.

This guidebook leads to many of the most distinctive and colorful beach communities in L.A. Each of the thirteen walking tours encourages the citywalker to actively explore the coastal villages, to interact with the urban setting. Beginning with a brief introduction to the community's geography, history, and character, each tour starts with breakfast at a lively local cafe. Then it leads through the community's most unique neighborhoods, encountering various points of interest, including significant architecture, flora, cafes, stores, landmarks, and even residents. A list of further reading concludes each chapter.

The Beach Towns: A Walker's Guide to L.A.'s Beach Communities differs from other Los Angeles guidebooks in two very important ways. First, it focuses upon walking in a car-oriented city. The tours are designed so that the citywalker experiences the best of Los Angeles as a whole urban environment. Each village is explored as a place of history, geography, culture, lifestyle, and art. Leading to the most captivating but often hidden places in beach towns, each tour not only explores the village along broad avenues and boulevards, but also via shady lanes, hillside stairways, quiet footpaths, parkside paths, oceanfront promenades, and canalside trails.

Second, the walks lead to the real character of L.A.'s beach villages. Each tour asks, ''What is the real spirit of this place? What gives Santa Monica or Venice its character and identity?'' By looking behind the scenes, be sensing the community's breath and heartbeat, by meeting the people and experiencing the whole cityscape, citywalkers encounter an in-depth, inside exploration of L.A.'s beach villages.

If you love citywalking, Los Angeles, the beach, or urban villages, then this book is written for you. If you've always wanted to know L.A. better or explore its coastline, then read on. A few additional guidelines are listed below to help you to get the most out of walking L.A.'s beach villages.

THE BEACH

The Beach: these two simple words paint sensuous pictures of Los Angeles as a semi-tropical paradise. Tanned bodies glistening with oil stretch lazily along miles of milk-white sands. Gentle ocean breezes rustle palms as daquiri-blue waves lap the shore. Yet the beach comprises more than these seductive images of the sun and surf.

Extending for seventy miles from mountainous Malibu to the shallows of San Pedro Bay, L.A.'s coastline includes a startling diversity of geography. Within this coastal region are wooded canyons, jagged sea cliffs, broad sandy beaches, rippled dunes, marshy wetlands, rocky points, terraced peninsula lands, rugged hills, and the world's largest manmade commercial and pleasure craft harbors.

The beach is endowed with Los Angeles' most pleasant climate. Ocean currents keep the summers cooler and the winters warmer. Constant sea breezes push air pollution inland, providing the beach villages with the region's cleanest air. With frequent early morning low clouds and cooler summer evenings, residents often carry light sweaters and windbreakers.

Because of its alluring climate and diverse geography, for hundreds of years all kinds of people have lived at the beach. In addition to surfers, sunbathers, and health fanatics, beach villagers range from working class families, middle class couples, and counterculture enthusiasts to nouveau riche glitterati, avant garde literati, emerging New Wavers, eccentric elderly, and the young of all ages. These people represent the ethnic and cultural diversity of Los Angeles.

These beach villages also contain nearly every kind of architectural style in Los Angeles. From weathered Victorians and ancient sycamores, Spanish Revival retreats and spiny cacti, and Craftsman bungalows and gnarled oaks to glass-sheathed high-rises and towering palms and Post-modern residences and bonsai gardens, the beach walks lead to a delightful variety of imaginative structures and landscaping.

TIPS ON CITYWALKING

More and more people are citywalking as a means of recreation, exercise, self enrichment, and community pride. Walking brings you face to face with the city, allowing you to sense, understand, and enjoy places and landscapes which you've never really noticed before. To best enjoy citywalking, here are a few simple guidelines.

First, develop an open minded attitude. Don't be timid to explore cafes, wander into shops, or ask questions of local residents. Be willing to learn about new social worlds; recognize that cities are places where people believe, dress, act, eat, play, and live differently from one another.

Second, practice an etiquette of citywalking. Respect other people's privacy and property. It is appropriate to ask questions of shopkeepers and cafe owners, but honor the individual homeowners' privacy by viewing their homes and gardens from the public sidewalk.

Third, be streetwise. Crime obviously exists on city streets, but you can greatly minimize potential problems by following a few streetwise directions. Walk with a friend. Keep a low profile; don't wear conspicuous or expensive jewelry or carry wads of cash. Dress casually. If someone looks or acts threateningly, don't engage him or her socially; walk straight ahead and look disinterested, not worrisome. The only problems I've had in years of L.A. citywalking are from barking dogs (ignore them and walk away), sore feet (wear comfortable shoes), and occasional rain (dress for the weather). By and large, citywalking is very safe, particularly if you're streetwise.

Finally, be a healthy citywalker. Wear flat, comfortable shoes. Take sunglasses, and dress for the setting and the weather.

With this guidebook, L.A. is yours.

SANTA MONICA CANYON
AND RUSTIC CANYON WALK

Along much of L.A.'s coastline, steep, jagged cliffs rise suddenly above the shore. At many places deep canyons cut by winter streams break through the cliffs and lead to cool interior woodlands. An air of mystery and intrigue surrounds these barrancas. Lush foliage clings to the canyon walls, interspersed with Mediterranean-style villas, Spanish hideaways, and Craftsman-style bungalows. Within minutes you can walk from the hot sand into the cool shadows of forested arroyos.

Santa Monica Canyon, the deep gorge which divides Santa Monica from Pacific Palisades, carves out a wide opening in the rugged sea cliffs. Snaking through the mountains, Rustic Canyon joins Santa Monica Canyon one-half mile from the ocean. A flat mesa is created between the two canyons, and for centuries people from pre-Columbian Indians to countrified urbanites have been drawn to this restful setting of babbling brooks, wooded hillsides, and dramatic views.

The canyons have a long and varied history. For over 8,000 years, Shoshone and Chumash Indians inhabited the region, thriving on abundant food sources in both the sea and the spring-fed canyons.

In 1542 the first Europeans arrived in Santa Monica Bay. Juan Rodriguez Cabrillo anchored offshore for one night but did not venture inland. For nearly 250 years afterwards, the region remained untouched by European explorers. Only the yearly passage of Spanish galleons sailing from Manila to Acapulco down the California coast drew the attention of the native Americans.

The Portola expedition of 1769 brought the first Europeans into Southern California. Searching for a legendary passageway from the Pacific to the Atlantic, as well as surveying the land for settlement, the expedition explored the Los Angeles area. The Spanish remained to colonize the region. Missions were built, Indians subjugated, and ranchos established.

SANTA MONICA CANYON
AND RUSTIC CANYON WALK

1. Stairpath
2. Mabery Road
3. Bradbury House
4. Norman House
5. Craftsman Style House
6. Patrick's Roadhouse
7. Les Anges Restaurant
8. Friendship Bar
9. Yellow House Cafe
10. Short Street and Channel Lane
11. Uphold House
12. Pedestrian Path
13. Craftsman House
14. Stairpath
16. Forestry Station
17. Uplifters Club
18. Kley House
19. Log Cabin Retreat
20. Log Cabin Retreat
21. Craftsman Style Cottage
22. Ranch House
23. Craftsman Style Cottage

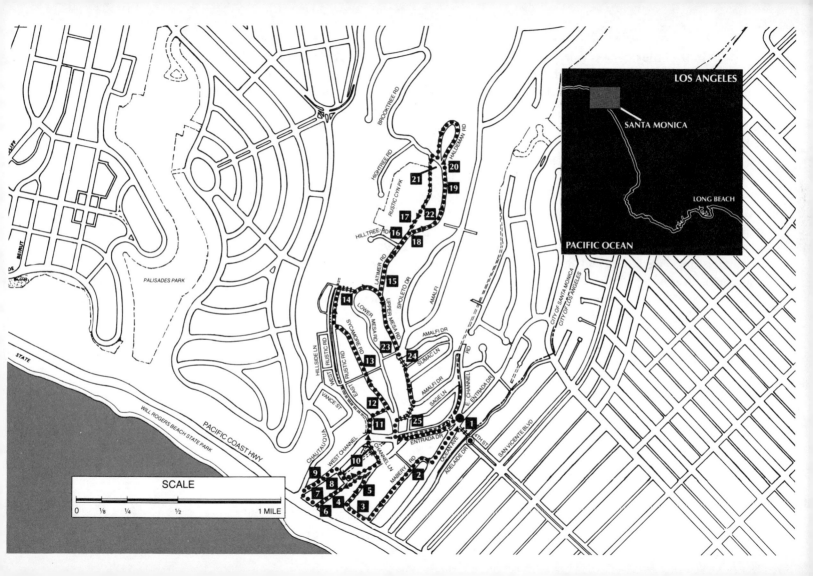

SCALE

0 ⅛ ¼ ½ 1 MILE

LOS ANGELES

SANTA MONICA

LONG BEACH

PACIFIC OCEAN

PACIFIC OCEAN

PALISADES PARK

WILL ROGERS BEACH STATE PARK

PACIFIC COAST HWY

RUSTIC CYN PK

BROOKTREE RD

HIGHTREE RD

HALDEMAN RD

HILLTREE RD

LATIMER RD

SPOLETO DR

AMALFI

AMALFI DR

AMALFI DR

SUMAC LN

SAGE LN

E. CHANNEL RD

ENTRADA DR

E. ENTRADA DR

SAN VICENTE BLVD

CITY OF SANTA MONICA

CITY OF LOS ANGELES

7TH ST

OCEANTANE

ADELAIDE DR

MABERY RD

CHANNEL LN

WEST CHANNEL

CHAUTAUQUA

VANCE ST

HILLSIDE LN

RUSTIC RD

WEST RUSTIC RD

EAST RUSTIC RD

SYCAMORE RD

LOWER MESA RD

UPPER MESA RD

STATE

In 1821 Mexico won independence from Spain. After an eighteen year legal dispute, a Mexican land grant in 1839 officially deeded these lands to two men, Ysidro Reyes and Francisco Marquez. Since 1831 Marquez had lived and worked in Santa Monica Canyon. And in 1835 Reyes had built a house on the western rim of Canada de Casa Vieja (Rustic Canyon) and owned a second adobe near Seventh Street and Adelaide.

The arroyos remained sparsely settled until the 1860's, when Santa Monica Canyon became a popular resort for vacationing Angelenos. A hotel was built in 1872 along with campsites, stables, and a bathhouse; day visitors and campers frequented the placid arroyos and enjoyed the cool ocean breezes.

Over the next few decades, the canyons served many purposes. Many saloons sprouted in lower Santa Monica Canyon, catering to a rough crowd of seafarers, dockworkers, and ranchers. In 1887 Abbot Kinney began the nation's first experimental forestry station in Rustic Canyon. Along the western bluffs of the arroyo, a fashionable residential area was platted by Kinney and developed by Collis Huntington in 1891, later called the Huntington Palisades. Large homes were built along the eastern edge as well. But the inner barrancas remained rural.

Today Santa Monica and Rustic Canyons are more densely populated, but they maintain their air of mystery and romance. This walk takes you into both canyons. It will guide you down stairpaths, over bridges, along narrow lanes, before log cabins and Italian villas, beneath the leafy shadows of alders, oaks, redwoods, and sycamores, and up steep stairpaths, introducing you to some of L.A.'s most hidden villages.

SANTA MONICA CANYON AND RUSTIC CANYON WALK

DIRECTIONS:	*Take I-10 (Santa Monica Freeway) west; exit Fourth Street right (west). Follow Fourth Street about fifteen blocks to Adelaide Drive.*
PARKING:	*Adelaide and Fourth generally have ample street parking.*
PUBLIC TRANSPORTATION:	*RTD lines 22, 322.*
DISTANCE:	*A hilly two miles with numerous stairpaths and steep lanes.*
DURATION:	*A meandering four hours, including breakfast and rests.*
SUGGESTED ITINERARY:	*Begin at the top of the Fourth Street stairs at Adelaide Drive in Santa Monica. Start early and stop for breakfast at the boisterous Patrick's Roadhouse or the quaint Yellow House.*
CLOTHES:	*Flat comfortable shoes, light casual wear, and perhaps a sweater.*

As Mabery Road winds into lower Santa Monica Canyon, it passes by many Spanish style houses, including this contemporary residence.

LOWER SANTA MONICA CANYON

Against a backdrop of apartment towers and condo high-rises, single family homes cling to the canyon's scraggly walls. For thousands of years, Indians encamped at this arroyo's mouth. In the last two centuries, the area has hosted grazing lands, campsites, saloons, bohemian retreats, and the present village of small businesses and hillside villas.

In the 1930's and '40's, the arroyo became the refuge for many artists, writers, and actors. Renowned residents included writer Christopher Isherwood, photographer Edward Weston, fashion photographers Peter Stackpole and Herbert

Matter, sculptors Holger and Helen Jackson and Merrill Gage (famous for his busts of Lincoln and his Academy Award winning 1955 short film "The Face of Lincoln"), and architect Thorton Abell.

Today, the lower canyon carries a mood of mixed lifestyles, casual tolerance, and friendliness.

1. **Stairpath**
   Fourth Street at Adelaide Drive
   Originally, a steep wooden stairway built in the 1920's allowed pedestrian access from the upper mesa to the lower canyon. In 1982 these well designed cement steps were laid, replacing the worn, rickety wooden ones. Now the path is a popular challenge to joggers and walkers alike. From this vantage point at the rim of the canyon, a magnificent vista encompasses the Santa Monica Mountains, the Malibu coast, the Pacific, and both Santa Monica and Rustic Canyons. Walk down the stairpath to Ocean Avenue.

2. **Mabery Road**
   between Ocean Avenue and Ocean Way
   Along this quiet road, squat houses compete for ocean and canyon views. Most of these residences were built in the 1920's and '30's and reflect that period's fascination with Mediterranean Revival architecture. Notice the white-washed walls, arched openings, and low pitched, terra cotta tiled roofs.

OCEAN WAY
between Mabery Road and Entrada Drive

A panorama of the Pacific coastline astonishes the walker at the cliff-edged turn of Ocean Way. Immediately below, traffic rumbles along the asphalt ribbon affectionately known as PCH (Pacific Coast Highway). To the west PCH leads to Malibu, a long sliver of coastal development known for its seafront mansions, perilously perched above the roaring waves. Looking southwest, the soft curve of Santa Monica Bay leads to Palos Verdes Peninsula, twenty miles away. On sunny days hundreds of boats sail the breezy bay, streaming out of Marina del Rey, seven miles south. As this lane gently descends into the canyon, the houses exhibit greater stylistic diversity. A few of the more notable structures are listed below.

3. **Bradbury House** (1922)
   102 Ocean Way
   The Bradbury House, designed by noted local architect John Byers, is a Spanish Colonial Revival adobe house with a bold tiled entrance.

4. **House**
   129 Ocean Way
   A two-story Norman cottage, accentuated with sculpted doorposts and magnolias.

5. House

150 Ocean Way

A classic Craftsman Style house, chateau-esque with its extended eaves, wide horizontal windows and shingled sidings.

SANTA MONICA CANYON COMMERCIAL DISTRICT
between Pacific Coast Highway and Short Street

A hodgepodge of bikini shops, bars, hardware stores, and cafes creates a jumbled business section, including the following:

6. Patrick's Roadhouse

102 Entrada Drive

Stop for breakfast in this landmark cafe. Inside, a juke box blares music as Bill Fischler, the uproarious owner, greets customers with infectious rowdiness. The motley decor might best be described as "British nautical kitsch," with its hanging cockleshell table lamps and old portraits of Victorian matrons. Order the "Bauernfruehstueck," an overstuffed omelette with everything *and* the kitchen sink.

7. Les Anges Restaurant

14809 Pacific Coast Highway

French provincial cuisine in an elegant minimalist setting; dinner only.

8. Friendship Bar

112 West Channel Drive

The oldest pub in the canyon, boasting the second oldest beer license in Los Angeles County, is anchored to the sidewalk by the salvaged wooden bow of a ship storm-wrecked in 1938. Inside, the rudder bears the engraved signatures of Doc Law, the original pub owner, and his famous cohort, Will Rogers.

9. Yellow House

147 West Channel Drive

A quaint, friendly restaurant specializing in seafood and healthy salads. The cinnamon swirl French toast, Belgian waffles, and Sunday champagne brunch are praised by locals.

10. Short Street and Channel Lane

After several harsh winter storms deluged the lower canyon (including the devastating flood of March 1938), in 1940 the WPA channelled the Santa Monica Creek with this cement conduit. This two-lane bridge provides clear views of the waterway.

Be extra careful crossing West Channel Drive with its speeding traffic.

LOWER RUSTIC CANYON

From the log cabin on the corner of East Rustic Road, you are reminded of a mountain village. For centuries the ancient sycamore trees have shaded the canyon floor. Early land deeds included covenants protecting these trees, and when this section was subdivided in 1913, the developers carefully built the roads and houses around the sycamores, preserving their charm for the neighborhood.

Since the 1920's, this secluded enclave has attracted a vibrant collection of creative people. In his book *A Single Man,* Christopher Isherwood aptly described this community's character:

> More probably the name was chosen for its picturesqueness by the pioneer escapists from dingy downtown Los Angeles and stuffy-snobbish Pasadena who came here in the early twenties. . . . Their utopian dream was of a sub-tropical English village with Montmartre manners: a Good Little Place where you could paint a bit, write a bit, and drink lots. . . . They were tacky and cheerful and defiantly bohemian, tirelessly inquisitive about each other's doings, and boundlessly tolerant.

Lower Rustic Canyon today continues to be a haven for artists and writers. The thick foliage, towering trees and countrified homes create a place where one can feel free to pursue personal dreams and activities.

11. Uphold House (1976)

320 East Rustic Road
Designed by architect Mark Wagner, this contemporary wooden residence is noted for its uneven lines, sharp angles, and secluded court. Landscape architect Sid Galper created the patio with brick flooring, a fountain, and an intricate latticed fence.

12. Pedestrian Path

between 322 and 326 East Rustic Road
Nearly hidden, this public passageway leads between two white posts to Sycamore Avenue, a narrow road with tidy cottages.

13. House

408 Sycamore Avenue
This 1920's Craftsman Style residence utilizes river boulders as a textured foundation.

14. Stairpath

between 546 and 550 East Rustic Road
From the bridge over Rustic Creek, view the middle canyon's cascading stream and wooded descent. Walk up the concrete path to the right of number 550; nasturtiums, fennel, and live oak embrace the stairway.

Weathered mailboxes, nailed to an old eucalyptus tree, attest to the rusticity of lower Rustic Canyon on Sycamore Road.

MIDDLE RUSTIC CANYON

Here Rustic Canyon widens and forms several terraced levels between the hillsides and the creek. Chaparral stubbornly hugs the steep arroyo walls, as sycamore, live oak, and eucalyptus grow near the spring-fed stream. Behind Himalayan deodar cedars and avocado trees, scores of whimsically styled residences reflect the changing architectural tastes of the past seventy years. Many canyon folk stroll along these lanes with a guarded enthusiasm about the enticing character of their hidden village.

15. Kaplan House (1973)

514 Latimer Road
Designed by Michael Leventhal, this wonderfully expressionistic house is embellished with handcrafted material, from the eccentric display of bricks for landscaping to the burlwood balconies and stained glass windows.

16. Santa Monica Forestry Station

Latimer Road between Hilltree Road and the Clubhouse
Abbot Kinney—tobacco magnate, amateur horticulturalist, connoisseur of the arts—persuaded the owners of Rustic Canyon in 1887 to donate six acres of terraced land for use as the nation's first experimental forestry station. For thirty-six years, hundreds of species of trees from around the world were planted to test their usefulness and adaptability to the geography and climate of coastal California. Although a fire destroyed most seedlings and structures in the station, today many rows of original stands remain to mark the station's earliest boundaries.

17. Uplifters Club

601 Latimer Road
In 1914 a splinter group of the staid Los Angeles Athletic Club organized to form an alternative, outlandishly irreverent club known as the Uplifters, dedicated to "uplift art, promote good fellowship, and build closer acquaintance among members." Several acres near the forestry station were purchased for a private clubhouse. By 1923 tennis courts, pool, stables, bridle paths, polo field, and outdoor amphitheater had been added. Soon additional acreage was bought to create a settlement of weekend hideaways and rustic retreats. Harry Marston Haldeman, grandfather of H. R. Haldeman of Watergate fame, and L. Frank Baum, author of the Oz books, led the club in the art of "High Jinx," which satirized high society of the '20's and '30's in songs, plays, and revelry. Members included such notables as Will Rogers, Harry Chandler, Busby Berkeley, Leo Carillo, Harold Lloyd, Ferde Grofe, and Darryl Zanuck. After World War II, many of the founders had died, and the Uplifters encountered financial difficulties. Land was gradually sold until 1953, when an anonymous philanthropist purchased the remaining property and donated it to Los Angeles as a public park and recreation center. Today, the Spanish Colonial Revival clubhouse is the park's center and offers a multitude of activities from fitness programs to educational classes.

HALDEMAN ROAD AND LATIMER ROAD

Many of the older homes along these lanes served as guest houses and summer retreats for the club's members. These residences were characterized by rustic motifs: shingled Craftsman cottages, rambling log-faced lodges, and a few authentic log cabins. Tucked into the lush hillsides, houses used river boulders as retaining walls and steps. As retreats became permanent residences, many cottages were remodeled, enlarged, and relandscaped, beautifully integrating the village into the wooded arroyo setting. Many noteworthy homes line these roads, and a few are described below.

18. **Kley House** (1923)
    1 Haldeman Road
    A rambling, graceful log-faced manor overlooks the canyon through ponderosa pines.
19. **Houses** (c. 1923)
    31, 32, and 33 Latimer Road
    These three log-faced cabins are camouflaged behind redwoods, nasturtiums, and bougainvillaea.
20. **Houses** (1923–24)
    36, 37, and 38 Latimer Road
    Banker Marco Hellman obtained these three log cabins from the set of the 1923 film ''The Courtship of Miles Standish.'' Constructed of whole logs, each cabin was disassembled on

Perched on the densely foliated canyon wall, the Marco Hellman log cabin overlooks Haldeman Road.

location near Lake Arrowhead and rebuilt on Hellman's lots. Number 38 was Hellman's personal retreat. Pasadena architect Arthur Heineman, who designed most of Hellman's banks, refashioned both the exterior and interior.

21. **House** (1922–23)

7 Haldeman Road

This elongated one-story Craftsman Style house with a variegated shingled roof evinces a rustic Scottish character.

22. **House**

4 Haldeman Road

A massive Moreton Bay fig tree shades the property with its extensive, broad-leafed branches.

23. **House** (1924)

2 Haldeman Road

Johnny Weissmuller in the '40's and Lee Marvin in the '50's lived in this now remodeled Craftsman Style cottage.

UPPER MESA

As you climb Upper Mesa Road, magnificent vistas of lower Rustic Canyon and Santa Monica Canyon spread below you. Along the hillsides wild mustard, rye grass, and fennel thrive. At the top of the hill, Amalfi Drive leads to large estates on the mesa.

24. **House** (1983)

407 Upper Mesa Road

A stark, bold, modern residence of reinforced concrete, its walls textured in rough lines and precarious angles, this house was designed by architect Robert A. Jackson. To the right, a stairpath leads down the steep hillside and affords another dramatic view of the house.

25. **Stairpath**

395 Upper Mesa Road

Descend this obscure stairway, shaded by Canary Island date palms, dense ficus, and acrid eucalyptus.

26. **Stairpath**

between 271 and 275 Amalfi Drive

Passing by small houses, walk to another nearly hidden stairpath. At the bottom, turn right to descend one final stair to Mesa Road. Return to the Fourth Street stairs and climb to Adelaide.

For Further Reading on Santa Monica Canyon and Rustic Canyon:

Fred E. Basten, *Santa Monica Bay: The First 100 Years,* 1979
Christopher Isherwood, *A Single Man,* 1957
Betty Lou Young, *Pacific Palisades: Where the Mountains Meet the Sea,* 1983
Betty Lou Young, *Rustic Canyon: The Story of the Uplifters,* 1981

Only half a mile from the ocean, Brooktree Bridge crosses over Rustic Creek. Oaks, sycamores, alders, and coast redwoods create a canopy over the spring-fed brook.

SANTA MONICA WALKS

Santa Monica offers the best of all worlds. Miles of broad beaches attract hundreds of thousands of sunbathers each year. Nostalgic Santa Monica Pier preserves the honky tonk '20's with its funky arcades, landmark carousel, and seaside carnival. Overlooking the vast Pacific, Palisades Park provides walkers and lovers shady paths and secluded beaches. In the skylit, high-tech Santa Monica Place, shoppers browse among the latest fashions and sample sushi, baklava, and chocolate-dipped strawberries. And in smoky pubs, Anglophiles guzzle pints of Watney's as they cheer dart throwing contests. Among all of L.A.'s beach cities, none compares to the cosmopolitan and sophisticated character of Santa Monica.

Yet only 150 years ago, the city was barren scrubland. Bordered on the west by the azure Pacific, sandy beaches ended at jagged palisades, steep cliffs rising suddenly a hundred feet above the ocean. To the north, the area abruptly stopped at Santa Monica Canyon, a wooded arroyo leading into the mountains. And to the south, another barranca divided the mesa, opening at present-day Pico Boulevard and Ocean Front Walk. Inland, gentle rolling hills and shallow valleys were covered with wild grasses and a few oaks. Now the 8.1 square mile area has been completely urbanized with 95,000 residents.

In 1769, alarmed by reports of English and Russian explorations, the Spanish sent Gaspar de Portola and a small entourage from Mexico to colonize California by establishing a chain of missions and military posts between San Diego and Monterey. According to legend, the Portola Expedition encamped at the springs near University High School in west L.A. Father Juan Crespi held mass that day in honor of Santa Monica, a pious woman who cried incessantly for her heretical and wayward son. After years of sorrow and prayer, her son was converted and became the revered Saint Augustine. The clear waters of the springs reminded Father Crespi of Santa Monica's tears and he christened the grassy mesa after this faithful woman.

After Mexico won independence from Spain in 1821, the California territories were divided into large ranchos. The broad grasslands of Santa Monica were granted to Don Francisco Sepulveda in 1828 and extended inland to Westwood. Sepulveda raised cattle on the spring-fed mesa.

In 1872, Colonel Robert S. Baker, an enterprising sheep rancher from Kern County, visited Sepulveda's rancho and decided that the grassy mesa would be ideal for raising sheep. He paid $55,000 for 30,000 acres. After surveying the area, Baker realized the tremendous potential of Santa Monica as a terminus for the transcontinental railroad. With several wealthy backers, he laid plans for building a wharf, railroad, and town.

Baker's plans remained on paper until 1874, when another ambitious entrepreneur arrived in Santa Monica. John P. Jones, a wealthy senator from Nevada, had made a fortune from silver mining. Together, Jones and Baker platted a townsite, built a wharf, and laid plans for a railroad.

On July 15, 1875, Santa Monica's first public land auction was held. Over 4,000 spectators from both San Francisco and Los Angeles attended. The well publicized auction was a success. Within a year, over 900 residents and 160 structures occupied the town. By 1876 Baker and Jones had laid sixteen miles of the Los Angeles and Independence Railroad (L.A. & I.) from Santa Monica to Los Angeles, then only a small settlement of 8,000 people. Plans were announced for further rail expansion north through El Cajon to the mining town of Independence and eventually to Salt Lake City. The L.A. & I. hoped to break the near monopoly of Collis Huntington's Southern Pacific Railroad.

However, a financial panic in 1877 depleted Jones' Comstock Securities and silver wealth. The L.A. & I. had cost the senator a million dollars, and he was forced to sell the rail venture to Huntington at one-sixth his investment. Huntington, unwilling to compete against his own commercial port at Wilmington, tore out Santa Monica's wharf and limited its rail line to excursions.

As Los Angeles mushroomed in the 1880's, Southern Pacific reassessed Santa Monica as a commercial port. In 1892 the S.P. built an enormous wharf at the mouth of Potrero Canyon, one mile west of Santa Monica. Christened the Port of Los Angeles, the wharf stretched 4,750 feet and was the longest dock in the world. Santa Monica renewed its dream of becoming the major seaport of Los Angeles.

In 1897, however, the federal government designated San Pedro as the region's official deep water harbor. While Santa Monica's long wharf continued as a busy port for several years, by 1921 its pilings had been torn out. Thus, the city escaped massive commercial development and remained a residential and resort community.

The Pacific Electric's interurban trolley cars reached Santa Monica in 1896; thousands of Angelenos rode out every weekend to the cool oceanside city. Soon new piers were built for popular recreation and entertainment. Thrill rides, penny arcades, dance halls, bingo parlors, and cafes created the Coney Island of the West Coast.

In the 1920's, Santa Monica grew from a town of 15,000 to a city of 37,000. Exclusive clubs and palatial estates lined the beach below Palisades Park and became known as the "Gold Coast." New stores and businesses moved to the city. Donald Douglas set up an airplane factory in an old warehouse on Wilshire Boulevard. In 1924 the first around-the-world flight originated from Douglas' Cloverfield airport and made Santa Monica world famous.

During the 1930's and 1940's, the city continued to grow. The Douglas Aircraft Company employed thousands of area citizens. During World War II, Douglas became the leading manufacturer of military and commercial aircraft in California. The amusement piers continued to entertain Southern Californians as well as thousands of military service personnel.

While the city became more suburbanized in the 1950's, two public projects in the 1960's had tremendous effects upon Santa Monica. In 1965 three blocks of Third Street between Wilshire Boulevard and Broadway were redeveloped into a pedestrian shopping mall, revitalizing the commercial core of downtown. Then in 1966 the western terminus of the Santa Monica Freeway was completed, making the city's beaches and businesses more accessible to Southern Californians.

Since 1970 Santa Monica has undergone many startling changes, some politically controversial and others architecturally notable. Tom Hayden's Campaign for Economic Democracy and the liberal renters' rights majority on the city council have attracted widespread media coverage since 1977. Frank O. Gehry's innovatively designed Santa Monica Place and other structures have received numerous architectural awards. Modern high-rises have transformed the central city into a stylishly urbane setting. Santa Monica continues to experience renewal and enthusiasm as it faces its second century.

This chapter explores Santa Monica via two walks. The first rambles through downtown, leading you to Victorian cottages, English pubs, French cafes, New Wave clothing stores, historical landmarks, and sleek high-rises. The second walk explores Palisades Park and several of Santa Monica's finest residential neighborhoods, and describes the area's predominant types of trees and shrubs. Each walk encourages you to mingle with the cityscape and people of the "zenith city on the sunset sea."

DOWNTOWN SANTA MONICA WALK

1. Statue of Santa Monica
2. Lawrence Welk Plaza
3. Cafe Casino
4. Wilshire Palisades Building
5. Shangri-La Hotel
6. Gussie Moran House
7. Belle-Vue French Restaurant
8. Ye Olde King's Head Pub
9. Mayfair Theater
10. Crocker Bank Building
11. Santa Monica Mall
12. Keller Block
13. Cheshire Fox Inn
14. Rapp's Saloon
15. Out of the Past
16. L.A. Woman
17. The Inner Works
18. NaNa
19. Santa Monica Pier
20. Paseo Del Mar
21. Santa Monica Place
22. Builders Exchange Building
23. Lido Apartments
24. Office Building
25. Central Tower Building
26. Maya
27. Bruns Multiprises
28. Tudor House
29. Shanta Cuisine of India
30. HiDeHo Comics
31. Santa Monica Public Library
32. Thistle Flower of Scotland
33. U.S. Post Office
34. Pacific Bookstore
35. Zucky's
36. First Federal Savings Building
37. St. Augustine's By-The-Sea Episcopal Church
38. Arizona Avenue Open Air Market
39. Criterion Theater
40. Historical Foundation
41. Commercial Building
42. California Federal Building
43. Michael's
44. Huntley Hotel and Pancho Villa Restaurant
45. Miramar Sheraton Hotel

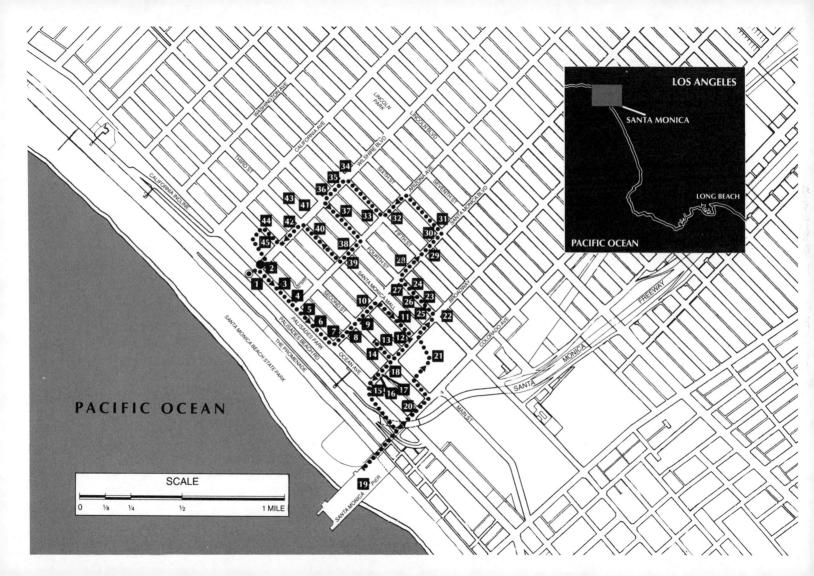

DOWNTOWN
SANTA MONICA WALK

DIRECTIONS: *Take I-10 (Santa Monica Freeway) west; exit right (west) on Fourth Street. Turn left on Wilshire Boulevard and follow to Ocean Avenue.*

PARKING: *The city of Santa Monica maintains six multi-level parking structures on Second and Fourth Streets between Wilshire and Broadway. Each structure offers free parking for three hours.*

PUBLIC
TRANSPORTATION: *RTD lines 4, 20, 22, 304. Santa Monica bus lines 1, 77, 10.*

DISTANCE: *Two and a half miles.*

DURATION: *An easy, adventurous, oh-let's-look-in-this-store three hours.*

SUGGESTED
ITINERARY: *Start at Ocean Avenue and Wilshire Boulevard, and have a mid-morning weekday breakfast at Cafe Casino. Wednesdays are ideal times to walk, with businesses open and the Arizona Avenue open air market bustling.*

CLOTHES: *Anything from Ocean Pacific shorts to Calvin Klein casuals.*

OCEAN AVENUE
between Colorado Avenue and Adelaide Drive

One of California's most picturesque boulevards, wide Ocean Avenue edges Palisades Park for nearly two miles. Canary Island date palms, condominium towers, office high-rises, and a few turn-of-the-century residences line its eastern side.

When Santa Monica was first settled, Ocean Avenue became the city's most prestigious address. Wealthy Angelenos, attracted by its magnificent ocean views, built large estates north of Wilshire. Wide sidewalks were set away from the tree-lined street to encourage quiet promenades and evening strolls. Even today, with its rich diversity of architecture, Ocean Avenue continues to allure pedestrians from every walk of life.

1. **Statue of Santa Monica** (1934)
   Ocean Avenue at Wilshire Boulevard
   Sculpted by Eugene Morahan, this cement statue of the city's namesake faces Wilshire Boulevard, the major highway to downtown Los Angeles. Standing in a heart-shaped lawn, Saint Monica prays for her son, Saint Augustine.
2. **Lawrence Welk Plaza** (1969)
   100 Wilshire Boulevard at Ocean Avenue
   Architects Daniel, Mann, Johnson, Mendenhall designed both the twenty-two story General Telephone Building and the adjacent sixteen-story Champagne Tower Apartments. Both structures are owned by Lawrence Welk, the famous

bandleader long associated with the Aragon Ballroom at the now-demolished Ocean Park Pier. The red metal sculpture in the Champagne Tower courtyard is by Peter Stein.

3. Cafe Casino
1299 Ocean Avenue

This popular French-style bakery and cafeteria offers both indoor and outdoor dining. The glass-enclosed patio, with its white umbrellas and furniture, overlooks Ocean Avenue and Palisades Park, attracting casual diners year round.

4. Wilshire Palisades Building (1981)
1299 Ocean Avenue

This thirteen-story terraced high-rise by Arthur Gensler and Associates has received numerous awards for its sharply angled, tiered design. With its royal palms, broad lawn, sunken amphitheater, cozy ledges, cascading stream, and adjoining patio at Cafe Casino, the superb landscape design encourages people to mingle and relax. The structure's overall scheme is beautifully and sensitively integrated with the Lawrence Welk Plaza and the Shangri-La Hotel.

5. Shangri-La Hotel (1940)
1301 Ocean Avenue

A seven-story reinforced-concrete hotel designed by William E. Foster in 1939, the Shangri-La Hotel reflects the period's interest in the machine aesthetic of aerodynamic design. With its banded, curved surfaces, steel railings, and balconies

Downtown Santa Monica's high-rises tower above passersby along Ocean Avenue. Cafe Casino, at the base of the Wilshire Palisades Building, provides an inviting setting for casual dining and people watching.

suggesting promenade decks, the hotel resembles a sleek ocean liner overlooking Ocean Avenue. The Shangri-La is one of several outstanding Streamlined Moderne structures in the city.

6. **Gussie Moran House** (ca. 1895)
   1323 Ocean Avenue
   This late Queen Anne Style Victorian house typifies the kind of beach residences which once lined Ocean Avenue and crowded Ocean Park. Number 1333 is another grand turn-of-the-century house, now converted into offices.

7. **Belle-Vue French Restaurant**
   1359 Ocean Avenue
   This family-run country French restaurant has been a local landmark for over forty years. Specializing in fresh seafood, the Belle-Vue prepares entrees from barracuda and mussels to Pacific red snapper to lobster, all caught locally in the Santa Monica Bay. The cozy interior features a collection of intriguing photos of old Santa Monica. The Friday bouillabaisse is first rate.

DOWNTOWN
bounded by Wilshire Boulevard, Ocean Avenue, Colorado Avenue, and Seventh Street

The oldest section of Santa Monica, downtown is the major commercial district of the city. Its architecture represents every decade of the city's growth since 1875. Ancient masonry buildings border Zigzag Moderne stores and Spanish Colonial offices face modern glass-sheathed towers, creating an exciting setting of architectural diversity.

This walk leads to many of the area's most unique cafes and shops, including most of Santa Monica's English pubs and tearooms. Significant architecture is also highlighted; as you walk, be sure to look up at the detailed ornamentation on many structures.

8. **Ye Olde King's Head Pub**
   120 Santa Monica Boulevard
   The oldest operating pub in Santa Monica, the King's Head is a popular gathering place for many types of British folk, including journalists, immigrants, and tourists from throughout the Commonwealth. Owners Phil and Ruth Elwell consider their public house ''not architecture, but a living thing; it's people from celebrities to painters.'' Unlike the segregated pubs in England or the darker bars in American cities, the King's Head is a lively, rowdy, boisterous place where people of all backgrounds chatter and jabber with one another. Whether downing a Guinness or throwing darts, Anglophiles pack the King's Head, especially on weekends. Next door the pub offers a wide range of traditional English dishes, from Welsh rarebit, Cornish pasties, and Scotch eggs to sherried Midland trifle, steak and kidney pies, and the specialty, fish and chips.

9. **Mayfair Theatre** (1911)
   214 Santa Monica Boulevard
   Designed by Henry C. Hollwedel, this small, informal theater presents many popular musicals, plays, and shows. Its

elaborate stone entry, dark wooden interior, and red velvet seats creat a cozy, intimate setting. Restored in 1973, the Mayfair claims to be "the oldest legitimate theatre operating in Los Angeles."

10. Crocker Bank Building (1930)

225 Santa Monica Boulevard
Designed by Stiles O. Clements, this subdued Zigzag Moderne high-rise resembles a fortified tower with its turreted parapets. For a quarter of a century the structure was Santa Monica's tallest building with its landmark clock tower.

11. Santa Monica Mall (1964–65)

Third Street between Wilshire Boulevard and Broadway
These three blocks were upturned and re-landscaped in 1964–65, transforming Santa Monica's busiest commercial street into a pedestrian mall. Designed with brick and tiled walkways, benches, and fountains, planted with South African coral trees and Australian eucalyptus, the Mall is a pleasant place to shop and stroll.

12. Keller Block (1892)

northwest corner of Third Street and Broadway
This weathered three-story brick building, once used as a hotel, now stands empty in its top floors, but houses an army-navy surplus store on the ground floor.

Zigzagging angles and alternating strips of smoked glass and concrete create a forceful modern design in the First Federal Savings Building at 401 Wilshire Boulevard.

13. Cheshire Fox Inn
1449 Second Street

Another busy hangout on weekends, this pub offers Anglophiles another taste of British life, but it is smaller and less lively than the King's Head. Its inexpensive cafe provides a wide range of English specialties, from simple baked beans on toast to beef wellington.

14. Rapp's Saloon (1875)
1438 Second Street

Designated an official Santa Monica city landmark in 1975, the historical marker reads, "This building, the first brick structure in the city, was erected in October 1875, as a tavern by William Rapp. . . . It served as a town hall from May 1887 to January 1889."

15. Out of the Past
130 Broadway

Stop inside this vintage clothing store for nostalgia buffs and say hello to Marv and Jeanie Reiner, the gregarious owners. Moved here from Hollywood in 1981, this collection specializes in 1930's and '40's apparel, including men's formal wear, women's velvet dresses, bowling shirts, kimonos, and hats.

16. L.A. Woman
126 Broadway

Owner Sally Bowl has been amassing antique and period women's wear since 1971. Her collection varies from Victorian dresses to '20's silk lingerie, '30's feathered hats, '40's chiffon and satin wedding dresses, and '50's floral gowns, as well as designer jewelry and original Maxfield Parrish posters. As you browse, ask Sally to play her Vera Lynn swing records.

17. The Inner Works
122 Broadway

A unique gallery of fine arts and crafts by women, specializing in ceramics, paintings, earrings, clothing, stationery, and books.

18. NaNa
120 Broadway

An offbeat assortment of '80's fashions, described by owner Paul Kaufman as "risky styles" from punk and rockabilly to new wave and nostalgic.

PALISADES PARK
between Broadway and Colorado Avenue

For over a century, this slender cliff-edged park has been a popular setting for strolling with friends, enjoying panoramic ocean views, and watching sunsets. Its winding paths lead through the arboretum to secluded benches, local monuments, and shady arbors. Along this stretch of the park, a diverse group of local and elderly folk use the special facilities, including a senior citizens' center and shuffleboard courts. The second walk in this chapter explores the section of Palisades Park north of Wilshire.

19. Santa Monica Pier

west end of Colorado Avenue
For a more detailed description of the pier and its attractions, see the Ocean Park Walk.

20. Paseo del Mar (1983)

1541–1551 Ocean Avenue
Designed by architects Prochnow and Frew, this attractive three-story Spanish Revival complex consists of four restaurants, fourteen shops, offices, and apartments. Two cafes offer outdoor dining: Croissant Show, an inexpensive cafe/bakery specializing in various croissant concoctions, and American Bar and Grill, a stylish, formal, moderately priced restaurant offering regional American dishes from New Orleans, New England, the Pacific Northwest, and the Southwest.

21. Santa Monica Place (1980)

bounded by Second Street, Broadway, Fourth Street, and Colorado Avenue
Designed by Frank Gehry and Associates, this three-level, skylit galleria creates an unconventional and inviting setting for 150 shops and two major department stores. Main entrances present dramatic Post-modern designs. Fountains, pools, tree-lined terraces, tiered levels, and bold angles all contribute to create an exciting people-oriented center. As you walk through the first-level lane leading in from the Broadway entrance, sample the smorgasbord of offerings ranging from stuffed potatoes, corn dogs, and kabobs to sushi, eigiku, burritos, souvlaki, spanakopita, and egg foo yung.

22. Builders Exchange Building (1928)

1505 Fourth Street
This four-story tower with its two-story wings exhibits the Churrigueresque style of Spanish Revival architecture, marked by elaborate ornamental panels of baroque Spanish designs set upon plain stucco surfaces.

23. Lido Apartments (ca. 1932)

1455 Fourth Street
This Classical Moderne brick building is bordered above by a line of seventeen indigo blue decorative figurines.

24. Office Building (ca. 1930)

1433–37 Fourth Street
Another example of the Churrigueresque style, although not as complex as the Builders Exchange Building.

25. Central Tower Building (1928)

1424 Fourth Street
Designed by Eugene Durfee, this eight-story Classical Moderne structure is accented with zigzag detailing. Unfortunately, the building lacks inspiration and sits heavily against the street. Note the ornamentation in the tile floors and entryway panels.

26. Maya

1428 Fourth Street
This trendy boutique stocks folk handicrafts from around the world, including L.A.'s largest selection of designer earrings (from Bali, Mexico, Thailand, and China) and a large collection of handwoven rugs (from India, Guatemala, and Afghanistan).

27. Bruns Multiprises

1422 Fourth Street

For over thirty years, the Bruns family has operated this musical instrument shop. Specializing in violins, violas, and cellos, Bruns has the largest collection of stringed instruments west of Chicago. One glance at the walls and you'll believe this claim: hundreds of violins of every shape and size hang in neat rows, each labeled by its year and maker. They range from fine master instruments costing thousands of dollars to the smallest of violins measuring only eight inches in length.

28. Tudor House

411 Santa Monica Boulevard

A bakery, grocery, and tearoom catering to British appetites, Tudor House offers a wide selection of savory foods. Its shelves contain fresh-baked scones, meat pies, and Scottish pasties. Imported jams, teas, and biscuits stock its grocery. And daily at 4 p.m., Tudor House hosts a traditional English tea, with sandwiches, crumpets, scones, and trifle.

29. Shanta Cuisine of India

502 Santa Monica Boulevard

In an elegant setting of linen, brass lanterns, handcarved shutters, and lush plants, Shanta presents a varied menu of authentic Indian cuisine. Their own tandoor oven bakes Northern Indian non-curried dishes, such as lobster tikka (''lobster tails marinated in delicate spices and fresh lemon and made with bell peppers, mushrooms, and tomatoes'').

30. HiDeHo Comics

525 Santa Monica Boulevard

Having collected over 500,000 comic books, HiDeHo's owner Mike Smith claims to have the West Coast's largest stock of comics. Ranging from *Batman* #1 (printed in 1939 and now selling for $3,500) to a variety of underground comics (Zap and the Freak Brothers), HiDeHo's collection attracts a throng of comic buffs, from kids to film studio researchers. Twice a year, HiDeHo sponsors the Santa Monica Graphic Arts Festival, usually with 35–40 world renowned cartoonists in attendance.

31. Santa Monica Public Library (1965)

1343 Sixth Street

This main city library provides spacious, modern facilities for its large collection of books (over 200,000 volumes), periodicals, documents, and pamphlets. Its balconied, skylit main reading room contains art galleries and historical photographs for public viewing.

32. Thistle Flower of Scotland

1301 Fifth Street

A lively Scottish pub with half-timbered ceilings, tartan wallpaper, and a large dance floor, Thistle Flower is popular on weekends, particularly for its Sunday afternoon Big Band dances.

33. **U.S. Post Office** (1937)

1248 Fifth Street

This one-story, reinforced-concrete Moderne building, designed by Neal A. Melick and Robert D. Murray, utilizes zigzag ornamentation with its sweeping vertical supports, accented with florid designs. Gnarled carob trees shade its sidewalk.

34. **Pacific Bookstore**

515 Wilshire Boulevard

In a noteworthy Streamlined Moderne building, this friendly neighborhood book shop is well stocked with best sellers as well as excellent books on local history, recreation, and outings.

35. **Zucky's**

northwest corner of Wilshire Boulevard and Fourth Street

A Santa Monica landmark, this twenty-four-hour eatery contains a busy restaurant, bakery, and delicatessen, serving homesick New Yorkers knishes, bagels, and halvah.

36. **First Federal Savings Building and Plaza** (1981)

401 Wilshire Boulevard

An imposing twelve-story contemporary office high-rise designed by Skidmore, Owings & Merrill, this dramatically angled building overlooks a wide pedestrian plaza, lined with trees and concrete trellises.

37. **St. Augustine's By-the-Sea Episcopal Church** (1969)

1227 Fourth Street

This modern church, designed by Daniel, Mann, Johnson, Mendenhall, replaced an older redwood church which burned in 1966. The new complex surrounds a tree-filled churchyard, wherein stands a rose granite baptismal font, dated 1888, from the original church.

38. **Arizona Avenue Open Air Market**

Arizona Avenue between Second Street and Fourth Street

Since 1982, farmers and growers from Ojai to Pearblossom have set up stalls to sell their produce once a week on these several blocks. Reminiscent of Boston's Quincy Market and L.A.'s Farmer's Market, this bustling open air produce center attracts thousands of shoppers from the Los Angeles area. You can find exceptional bargains here on everything from fresh apricots and Persian melons to snow peas and zucchini. *W, 9 a.m. – 5 p.m.*

39. **Criterion Theater** (1923)

northeast corner of Arizona Avenue and the Mall

From the ornamental facade of this theater, stone faces smile upon Santa Monica Mall shoppers.

40. Historical Fountain (1965)

1200 Block of the Mall

This octagonal fountain sculpted by Merrill Gage traces Santa Monica's history in eight pre-cast concrete panels. Beginning with Cabrillo's discovery of Santa Monica Bay in 1542, the panels lead to Spanish settlement, rancho life, city founding, seaside resorts, Douglas aircraft fame, and beach recreation in Santa Monica.

41. Commercial Building (ca. 1930)

301–313 Wilshire Boulevard

Decorative concrete panels of Zigzag and Regency Moderne design grace the upper sections of this building's facade.

42. California Federal Building (1975)

233 Wilshire Boulevard

Sheathed in smoked black glass, this nine-story office building is surrounded by a shady park of contoured lawns, brick walks, and coral trees.

43. Michael's

1147 Third Street

Almost hidden behind sandstone-colored walls and tinted windows, Michael's is one of the most provocative and expensive restaurants in town. Its contemporary California French cuisine, inspired by a medley of young, imaginative, and demanding chefs, uses only the very best ingredients wherever found, whether the salmon is from the Pacific Northwest or Norway or the fresh raspberries from Oregon or New Zealand. Michael's claims to have sparked California's pasta craze, making its own pasta served with French-inspired, light cream-based sauces. Another trend launched by its chefs are hot salads, such as the sauteed wild mushroom salad with roasted pine nuts and warm vinaigrette. Inside, the restaurant is garnished with a striking collection of modern paintings from such artists as Jasper Johns, David Hockney, and Richard Diebenkorn. A lush garden patio in a sunken courtyard offers quiet outdoor dining. Michael's is prohibitively expensive for the average citywalker, and reservations are necessary two weeks or more in advance.

44. Huntley Hotel and Pancho Villa Restaurant (1964)

1111 Second Street

The real treasure of this bland high-rise is its glass elevator, which slowly creeps up the hotel's exterior and affords a breath-taking panoramic view of Santa Monica Bay. Take the elevator to the top floor and visit Pancho Villa's, an inexpensive Mexican restaurant specializing in seafood and city views. At dusk you can sip peach margaritas and watch the sunset behind the Malibu coast.

45. Miramar Sheraton Hotel

101 Wilshire Boulevard

Originally this square block was the site of Senator John P. Jones' estate, built in 1888. Now the extensive hotel complex of brick buildings, dining and conference rooms, and semi-tropical landscaping attracts visitors from around the world. Walk through the lobby and out the Wilshire Boulevard exit to see the massive Moreton Bay fig tree planted in 1879 by Mrs. Jones. The broad-leafed tree was declared an official Santa Monica landmark in 1976.

NORTHWESTERN SANTA MONICA WALK

1. Senator Jones Memorial
2. George Hastings Memorial Garden
3. Cabrillo Monument
4. Viewing Arbor
5. Idaho Gates
6. ''The Gables'' Ruins and Mural
7. Inspiration Point
8. Alaskan Totem Pole
9. Ocean Towers Apartments
10. Roy Jones House
11. Minter House
12. Craftsman Style House
13. Holliday House
14. Gorham House
15. Stairpath
16. Craftsman Style House
17. Spanish Colonial Revival House
18. Stairpath
19. Grofe House
20. Fischman-Savett House
21. Bougainvillaea
22. Pueblo Revival House
23. Kaffirboom Coral Trees
24. Fourth Street Parkway
25. Craftsman Style House
26. Hart House
27. Southern Magnolia Trees
28. Byers House
29. Eucalyptus Trees
30. Goose Egg Park
31. Craftsman Style House
32. Witbeck House
33. Craftsman Style House
34. Mediterranean House
35. Housecourt
36. Riverton Place
37. Craftsman Style House
38. Tegner House
39. Sovereign Hotel
40. Embassy Apartments
41. Charmont Apartments
42. Brazilian Pepper Trees
43. Lemon Scented Eucalyptus Trees
44. Huntley Hotel

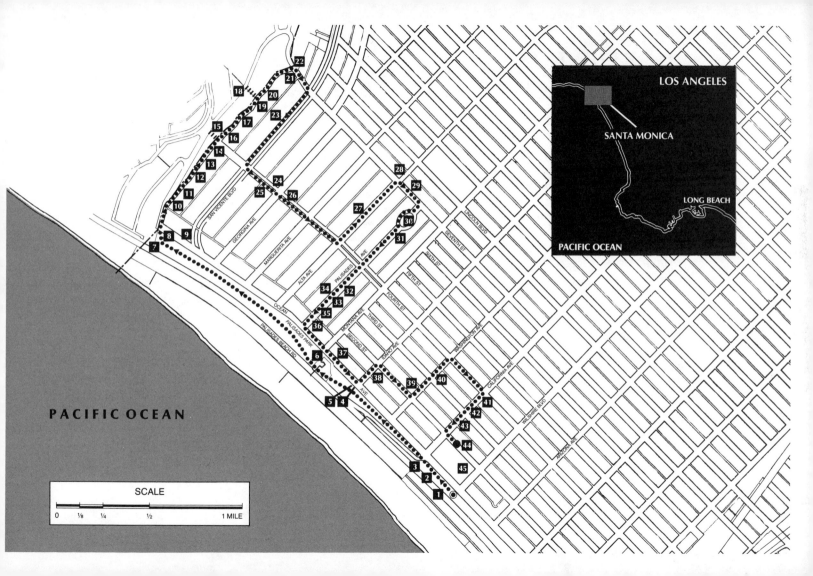

PACIFIC OCEAN

PACIFIC OCEAN

LOS ANGELES

SANTA MONICA

LONG BEACH

SCALE

0   ⅛   ¼   ½   1 MILE

NORTHWESTERN SANTA MONICA WALK

DIRECTIONS: *Take I-10 (Santa Monica Freeway) west; exit right (west) on Fourth Street. Turn left on Wilshire Boulevard and follow to Ocean Avenue.*

PARKING: *The city of Santa Monica maintains six multi-level parking structures on Second and Fourth Streets between Wilshire and Broadway. Each structure offers free parking for three hours.*

PUBLIC TRANSPORTATION: *RTD lines 4, 20, 22, 304. Santa Monica bus lines 1, 77, 10.*

DISTANCE: *A little over four miles.*

DURATION: *A briskly-paced three hours.*

SUGGESTED ITINERARY: *Start at Palisades Park across from Wilshire Boulevard. Have a late breakfast or brunch at Zucky's at Wilshire and Fifth. Conclude the tour with an early dinner or cool drink at Pancho Villa's Restaurant, 1111 Second Street.*

PALISADES PARK

With its panoramic view of Santa Monica Bay from Malibu to Palos Verdes, Palisades Park is one of California's most scenic and popular urban parks. The narrow green space stretches nearly two miles between the Municipal Pier and Santa Monica Canyon. Along its oceanside edge, jagged cliffs drop sharply to the Pacific Coast Highway a hundred feet below, affording unobstructed views of the seacoast.

For over a hundred years, Palisades Park has been a traditional place to take quiet afternoon strolls and to enjoy romantic sunsets. When Senator John P. Jones and Arcadia de Baker donated most of the parkland to the city in 1895, various plans were proposed for creating formal gardens and brick walkways. After years of debate and planning, Palisades Park gradually assumed its present design as an arboretum of trees, shrubs, and plants placed in rows and groves throughout the wide lawns. Over the decades, winding paths, historical monuments, shady arbors, picnic tables, secluded benches, and restrooms have been added.

On any sunny afternoon, hundreds of people laze in the park — reading, playing cards, picnicking, sunning, or contemplating. Others use the lawns and gardens more actively by jogging or playing frisbee. Listen carefully and you'll detect a score of languages and accents as people from throughout cosmopolitan Los Angeles enjoy Palisades Park.

1. **Senator Jones Memorial** (1923)

    opposite the Miramar Sheraton Hotel at Wilshire Boulevard
    This graceful concrete bench, overlooking the Pacific, marks
    the spot where Senator John P. Jones, one of the founders of
    the city, used to sit each evening and watch the sunset. Jones'
    estate, a large residence amid parklike grounds, was called the
    Miramar and stood where the hotel now stands.

2. **George Hastings Memorial Garden** (1963)

    north of Wilshire Boulevard
    This small garden, edged by a simple picket fence, honors
    George Hastings, founder of the Santa Monica Nature Club
    and author of *Trees of Santa Monica*. A resident of Santa
    Monica for over twenty years, Hastings dedicated himself to
    the identification, planting, and cultivation throughout the city
    of hundreds of trees and shrubs from around the world.

3. **Cabrillo Monument** (1949)

    at California Avenue
    A brass plaque set in a large granite boulder celebrates the
    400th anniversary of Juan Rodriguez Cabrillo's discovery in
    1549 of placid Santa Monica Bay.

    Just north of California Avenue stand stately rows of
    tall palms, resembling ancient temple columns. The tallest
    palms, marked by slender trunks and fanned leaves, are
    Mexican fan palms (*Washingtonia robusta*), native to Baja
    California. The thick-trunked palms with long, spiny leaves

For over a hundred years, cliff-edged Palisades Park has been a favorite
place to stroll at sunset. Narrow Washington palms tower above the
twisting paths.

(sometimes fifteen to twenty feet in length) and clusters of yellow-orange fruit are **Canary Island date palms** (*Phoenix canariensis*).

4. Viewing Arbor (ca. 1924)

near Idaho Avenue

This Craftsman Style wooden arbor, with resting and viewing benches, is surrounded by a number of unusual plants and trees. Native to the Canary Islands, a pair of **dragon trees** (*Dracaena draco*) resembling tall succulents rise above the arbor. The thick, heavy trunks are topped by several short bunches of dagger-shaped leaves. Several small, heavily foliated **karos** (*Pittosporum crassifolium*) shade the arbor with their thick gray-green leaves. Karos are easily identified by the felt-like texture of their dusty leaves and are native to New Zealand.

5. Idaho Gates (1917)

at Idaho Avenue

These twin Craftsman Style gates, anchored with large river boulders and broken bricks, are accented with delicate glazed tiles by Ernest Batchelder of Pasadena. Against the gates grow **lemon bottlebrush** (*Callistemon citrinus*). These bushy shrubs have cylindrical red blossoms which resemble bottle brushes. Crush a leaf and smell the lemony scent. Native to Australia, lemon bottlebrush lines many streets in Southern California. In the area on either side of the restrooms are groves of eucalyptus trees, also native to Australia. The medium trees with weeping branches and smooth upper bark are **red gums** (*Eucalyptus camaldulensis*). As with nearly all of the 300

species of eucalyptus, the leaves are sticky and have an acrid scent when crushed. Many eucalyptus oils, collected from leaves, have medicinal and balsamic uses.

6. "The Gables" Ruins and Mural (1928)

below the Montana Avenue Steps

The Montana Steps lead into an eroded opening in the Palisades and to the beach and an abandoned hotel site. In 1928 the foundation and the first two floors of the Gables Hotel were built, but the Depression forced the developers to abandon the project. In 1978 artist Jane Golden painted the mural of pre-Columbian Indian life along the Palisades coastline. Back in the park, north of Montana Avenue, the path leads through rows of lofty Mexican fan palms, jutting eighty-five feet into the sky. A circular garden of a dozen varieties of roses enriches the parkscape opposite Palisades Avenue.

7. Inspiration Point

northwest end of Palisades Park

At this spot in 1769, scouts from the Portola Expedition followed Indian guides and stopped to survey the Malibu coast. Returning to Portola, they reported that the northern coastal route was impassable. Now the dramatic view is, disappointingly, obstructed by a high-rise condominium tower.

8. Alaskan Totem Pole (1926)

opposite Adelaide Drive

Carved by the Chilkat Thlinger Alaskan Indians, this thirty-foot totem pole was donated to the city by J. Walter

Todd in 1926. Along Ocean Avenue, several **Hollywood junipers** (*Juniperus chinensis*) twist upward with their thick, clumpy foliage. Pinch their scaly leaves and smell the piney scent.

ADELAIDE DRIVE
between Ocean Avenue and Seventh Street

Since 1834, when Ysidro Reyes built an adobe near Adelaide Drive and Seventh Street, this winding road has been a secluded residential setting. Curving along the southwestern rim of Santa Monica Canyon, Adelaide Drive offers spectacular views of the Santa Monica Mountains, Pacific Palisades, Rustic Canyon, and the Pacific.

Most of the large homes here were built between 1905 and 1930, and reflect the popular architectural styles of the era. Excellent examples of Craftsman Style manors and Spanish Colonial Revival estates with well landscaped gardens peer into the canyon. Remote, private, and serene, Adelaide Drive is a perfect setting for peaceful strolls.

Because many of the residents frequently visit neighbors, stores, and the beach in the canyon below, two hillside stairpaths were constructed from Adelaide Drive down the steep canyon wall. These long flights of steps today are well used by the nearby community, particularly by joggers and citywalkers.

The stark face of the Ocean Tower Apartments contrasts sharply with the oriental features of Craftsman Style houses on Adelaide Drive.

9. **Ocean Tower Apartments** (1971)
201 Ocean Avenue
William Holden once lived in one of these twin seventeen-story apartment buildings designed by Krisel, Shapiro, and Associates. Their sheer bulk overshadows the smaller-scale single-family houses and two-story apartments nearby.

10. **Roy Jones House** (1907)
130 Adelaide Drive
A peculiar mix of Colonial American Revival and Craftsman styles, this house was the residence of Roy Jones, the nephew of Santa Monica's founder.

11. **Minter House** (1910)

    142 Adelaide Drive

    The California Craftsman movement integrated many forms of Oriental aesthetics into its architectural forms, evident here in the variegated eaves of the oversailing roof.

12. **House** (1915)

    236 Adelaide Drive

    An imposing two-story Craftsman manor, with wide brick walkways, broad rolling lawns, and well-manicured gardens.

13. **Holliday House** (1919)

    316 Adelaide Drive

    This adobe Spanish Colonial Revival house was built at a time when California was rediscovering its romantic rancho heritage. Balconies laced with iron grilles, thick adobe walls, terra cotta roof tiles, and arched openings distinguish this style.

14. **Gorham House** (1924)

    326 Adelaide Drive

    John Byers, a long-time Santa Monica resident and instructor at the City College, was a leading local architect who designed many Spanish Colonial Revival houses, including this dwelling set back from the street. Note the painted tiles around the door and the grille around the balconies.

15. **Stairpath** (1982)

    Fourth Street at Adelaide Drive

    These steep steps provide pedestrian access between the mesa cityscape and the canyon. Local residents frequently walk and jog these stairs to the beach, stores, and homes of friends in the canyon. In 1982, the city of Los Angeles designed and built these beautiful concrete steps to replace the rickety wooden stairpath built in the 1920's. Contrary to cynical urban myths about L.A., some public routes cater exclusively to citywalkers, not cars!

16. **House** (ca. 1910)

    406 Adelaide Drive

    This manorial, two-story Tudor Craftsman house was designed by noted architects Elmer Grey and Myron Hunt.

17. **House** (ca. 1927)

    436 Adelaide Drive

    Another Spanish Colonial Revival house, recently remodeled and relandscaped.

18. **Stairpath** (ca. 1935)

    opposite 526 Adelaide Drive

    Nearly hidden from the street, this wooden stairpath cascades down the bluff, leading to the Canyon Elementary School. A one-room schoolhouse built in 1894 may be seen on the school grounds.

19. **Grofe House** (ca. 1935)

    540 Adelaide Drive

    Ferde Grofe, the famous composer of the ''Grand Canyon Suite,'' lived here in the 1930's.

20. **Fischman-Savett House** (1940; remodeled 1978)

    640 Adelaide Drive

    Originally built in 1940, this house was remodeled and enlarged in 1978 by architect Mark Meryash, creating a Bauhaus-inspired structure marked by flat stucco walls, sixty-

and ninety-degree corner angles, and sheer facades void of accouterments. In the 1970's architect Cesar Pelli lived here while he designed the Pacific Design Center in Hollywood.

21. Bougainvillaea
642 Adelaide Drive

Intertwining the rough wooden fence, this red-flowered shrub with heart-shaped leaves grows throughout California. Its woody, thorny vines often creep into trees and arbors, creating canopies of brilliantly red and vermillion blossoms.

22. House (ca. 1925)
710 Adelaide Drive

An outstanding example of Pueblo Revival architecture, this flat-roofed house features soft stuccoed walls, rounded corners, and rough-hewn beams extending beyond the exterior walls, creating interesting shadows.

SAN VICENTE BOULEVARD
between Seventh and Fourth Streets

Once Pacific Electric trolley cars glided along San Vicente Boulevard between Westwood and Venice. When the tracks were uprooted in the 1940's, these gnarled South African coral trees were planted along the parkway. Now the landscaped center strips attract a myriad of joggers and urban hikers. This shady boulevard is one of the most desirable locations for apartment and condominium living in Los Angeles County.

23. Kaffirboom Coral Trees
San Vicente Boulevard between Ocean Avenue and Twenty-sixth Street

Native to South Africa, these sub-tropical trees (*Erthrina caffra*) have become local landmarks with their gnarled roots, heavy branches, and dense foliage. In the early winter, when the tree is bare of leaves, burnt orange blossoms blaze from the tips of branches, earning the colloquial name "fire coral trees."

Adelaide Drive winds along the edge of Santa Monica Canyon, affording panoramic views and a secluded setting.

PALISADES TRACT
bounded by San Vicente Boulevard, Ocean Avenue, Montana Avenue, and Seventh Street

First subdivided in 1905, the Palisades Tract offered spacious lots along wide avenues, encouraging the development of an affluent neighborhood. Many stately homes, some quietly impressive and others a bit grandiloquent, have been built over the past eighty years. Well manicured lawns and mature trees grace most estates and contribute to an aesthetically rich and architecturally interesting setting for citywalking.

24. Fourth Street Parkway

between San Vicente Boulevard and Montana Avenue
The original developers of the Palisades Tract designed this public parkway in 1905 as a public green, making the residential community more attractive for leisurely afternoon walks. Regal, slender **queen palms** (*Syagrus romanzoffianum*), native to Brazil, grace the center parkway with their long plume-like fronds, which sometimes reach fifteen feet in length. At the woody base of the fronds grow soft white flowers and yellow fruit. Along the sidewalks are **New Zealand Christmas trees** (*Metrosideros excelsa*), medium-sized bushy trees with burgundy-red flowers and felty leaves. Stringy vines hang underneath the branches.

25. House (ca. 1907)

325 Georgina Avenue
This two-story Craftsman Style house, with shingled sides and heavy wooden beams, is almost overshadowed by a huge

Italian stone pine (*Pinus pinea*), a rough-barked conifer with broad branches and a rounded crown. The tree, native to the Mediterranean region, has edible seeds with very hard shells, which give it the name of ''stone.''

26. Hart House (ca. 1840's)

404 Georgina Avenue
The oldest structure in Santa Monica, the original adobe section of this Spanish house dates to the 1840's and was used by Sepulveda's ranch hands as a dwelling when the grassy mesa was barren and windswept. For years this house has been owned by William S. Hart, Jr., the son of the famous silent film western actor.

27. Southern Magnolia Trees

Alta Avenue between Fourth Street and Seventh Street
Native to the southeastern United States, these stately trees (*Magnolia grandiflora*) have large glossy leaves which are jade green above and rust-colored underneath. The huge, creamy white flowers carry a fragrant scent.

28. Byers House (1917)

547 Seventh Street
The first house designed by local architect John Byers, this modest Craftsman Style house preceded Byer's intensive study of Spanish Colonial Revival design. Across the street at 624 Alta Avenue stands a Spanish-style house built by Byers in 1925.

29. Eucalyptus Trees (1876)

Seventh Street between San Vicente and Wilshire Boulevards
One year after the city's founding, J. W. Scott purchased forty-three acres of undeveloped land between Fifth Street and

Lincoln Boulevard in 1876. He planted over a thousand eucalyptus trees along Seventh Street, many of which shade the street today. Among these trees are two predominant species, **blue gums** and **yates.** The first *(Eucalyptus globulus)* grow up to 120 feet high, with a deciduous bark which peels off in long strips. In these older trees, the lower bark remains rough. Yates *(Eucalyptus cornuta)* grow to about fifty feet and have a rough, chocolate-brown bark marked by deep furrows. The leaves of both trees are sticky and acrid.

30. Goose Egg Park (1905)

Palisades Avenue between Seventh and Fourth Streets
Planned by the original developers in 1905, this oval-shaped public park refreshes the neighborhood with a delightful deviation from the gridded street pattern. A number of mature trees shade the park, including Canary Island date palms, a huge yate, and New Zealand Christmas trees. The towering conifer, an **Aleppo pine** *(Pinus halepensis),* is native to the Mediterranean region, and its age is marked by a ruggedly furrowed bark. The densely foliated trees with wavy-edged leaves are **orange pittosporum** *(Pittosporum undulatum),* an Australian tree with white, orange-scented clusters of flowers. Commonly planted in Los Angeles, these trees are often trimmed as hedges.

31. House (ca. 1915)

514 Palisades Avenue
A classic Craftsman Style house, characterized by a river boulder foundation and chimney, shingled sides, extensive veranda, and etched glass. Note the four old Canary Island date palms in the front, as well as a **coast**

redwood *(Sequoia sempervirens).* The tallest trees on earth, coast redwoods are native to the northern and southern California coast, where cool temperatures, moist air, and moderate rainfall nurture the trees. But in the drier, sunnier region of Southern California, coast redwoods often grow to be short and stubby. They are easily identified by the reddish, soft bark and small cones surrounded by thin, flat leaves.

32. Witbeck House (1917)

226 Palisades Avenue
Designed by noted architects Charles and Henry Greene, famous for their Pasadena Craftsman houses, this two-story, Tudor-style residence is delicately landscaped and beautifully maintained.

33. House (ca. 1915)

222 Palisades Avenue
A modest one-story house expressive of the low, shingled Craftsman style. Behind the latticed fence is a wide-spreading **Moreton Bay fig tree** *(Ficus macrophylla),* an Australian tree with sturdy buttressed roots, brownish leaves, and wide branches. The largest specimen in Santa Monica is the Founders Tree in the Miramar Sheraton Hotel courtyard, planted by Mrs. Jones in 1879.

34. House (ca. 1920; remodeled 1981)

215 Palisades Avenue
A wonderfully whimsical Mediterranean villa, with tiled walkways, walled front patio, spindled woodwork, carved wooden beams, trellised roof garden, and French doors leading into numerous balconies.

35. Housecourt (1922)

124–130 Palisades Avenue

Seven small bungalows of a simple English countryside styling face the central court.

OCEAN AVENUE
between Palisades and Idaho Avenues

36. Riverton Place (1932)

701 Ocean Avenue

Designed by Donald Parkinson, this quiet one-story housecourt is accented with latticed entries, adobe trim, and Hollywood junipers.

37. House (ca. 1919)

815 Ocean Avenue

This two-story Craftsman Style manor, chalet-esque with its flower boxes, wide overhanging roof, and dark wood, evokes an earlier era when grand houses lined Ocean Avenue.

WILSHIRE NORTH
bounded by Montana and Ocean Avenues, Wilshire Boulevard, and Seventh Street

Santa Monica's earliest residential neighborhood, Wilshire North was once crowded with Victorian cottages, Craftsman Style manors, and large estates. But during the past half-century, many multi-unit complexes have been built, replacing single-family homes with hotels, apartments, housecourts, and offices. Today, this neighborhood is densely populated, its architecture varying from grand Spanish hotels to ticky-tacky stucco apartments to a spattering of Craftsman houses.

38. Tegner House (1906)

918 Second Avenue

One of the few remaining late-Victorian houses in the community, this two-story residence was the home of Charles E. Tegner, a leading Santa Monica businessman in the first third of this century. Along Second Avenue grow **Indian laurel fig trees** *(Ficus microcarpa),* a commonly planted shade tree with glossy leaves, smooth ash-white bark, and thick foliage.

39. Sovereign Hotel (1929)

205 Washington Avenue

Typical of the popular Spanish Revival hotels which were built throughout Los Angeles in the 1920's, this five-story, thick-walled structure was designed by Meyer Radon.

40. Embassy Apartments (1927)

1001 Third Street

Another resort high-rise detailed with Spanish Revival motifs, this four-story building embraces a lush garden courtyard and features balconies with French doors and intricate iron grillwork.

41. Charmont Apartments (1922)

330 California Avenue

This grand five-story Spanish Revival apartment tower overlooks a central court with an elaborately tiled, tiered fountain, now converted into a flower garden. Look up and notice the zigzag detailing near the roof.

42. Brazilian Pepper Trees
320 California Avenue

A medium-sized tree *(Schinus terebinthifolius)* with dark, rough bark and twisting branches, it is named for the small white blossoms which form pepper berries, often dried and ground for use as spice. A **California Pepper tree** *(Schinus molle)*, which is identified by its weeping branches, thin lime-green leaves, and clusters of small red berries, may be found in front of Michael's Restaurant, 1147 Third Street.

43. Lemon Scented Eucalyptus Trees
222 California Avenue

Tall, graceful, and slender, sometimes reaching one hundred feet in height, these trees have a smooth bark with white and tan patches. When crushed, the narrow leaves have a lemony scent.

44. Huntley Hotel (1964)
1111 Second Street

Ride the glass elevator up to the rooftop Pancho Villa's Mexican restaurant for panoramic views of Santa Monica Bay and Malibu. After refreshments and perhaps an early dinner, walk back to Palisades Park for a sunset stroll.

The Sovereign Hotel at 205 Washington Avenue is typical of the many Spanish Revival structures built throughout Los Angeles in the 1920's.

For Further Reading on Santa Monica and Palisades Park:

Fred E. Basten, *Santa Monica Bay: The First 100 Years,* 1974
Raymond Chandler, *The Big Sleep,* 1939
Raymond Chandler, *Farewell, My Lovely,* 1940
George T. Hastings, *Trees of Santa Monica,* 1976
James Lundsford, *Looking at Santa Monica,* 1983
Santa Monica *Evening Outlook, A Century of History in Santa Monica, 1875–1975,* 1975
Leslie Storrs, *Santa Monica: Portrait of a City, Yesterday and Today,* 1974

OCEAN PARK WALK

Although politically an extension of Santa Monica, Ocean Park is worlds apart. Whereas Santa Monica tends to be conventional and sedate, Ocean Park shows vigor and charm as an urban village. Its old homes are being renovated, not replaced. In fact, walking in Ocean Park transports you to a turn-of-the-century beach village.

Abbot Kinney, before his ventures in Venice, joined with Francis Ryan and A. R. Fraser in 1892 to develop Ocean Park. At that time the area was largely a sandy expanse of hills and marshes, interspersed with several small farms. Purchasing a strip of oceanfront land, they platted a small seaside resort. The development grew in 1896 as a local interurban railway was extended from Santa Monica, allowing for quick, reliable, and inexpensive transportation.

By 1900 Ocean Park had grown to a village of over two hundred cottages. It had its own businesses, post office, golf course, auditorium, and race track. Fraser built a huge oceanfront bathhouse, complete with ornate domes and heated salt water plunge, which operated from 1905 to 1930.

During these decades Ocean Park attracted thousands of visitors to amble along its beachfront promenade, to frolic in the Pacific, and to play in its festive arcades.

Although Ocean Park continued to attract summer crowds during the Depression, each year saw fewer visitors and less revenue. During the 1940's and '50's, the character of the neighborhoods changed dramatically. Older families moved to newer suburbs. Property values dropped. A diverse mix of poorer people — the working class, the elderly, minorities, and avant garde intellectuals — settled in the aging resort.

In the late 1950's, Ocean Park and neighboring Venice became havens for Beatniks. Writers, poets, artists, and musicians found refuge in old bungalows and gathered in bohemian coffee houses. Lawrence Lipton chronicles this counterculture movement in his book *The Holy Barbarians*.

The most ambitious project ever undertaken in Ocean Park was begun in 1958 to attract beach crowds. Pacific Ocean Park (P.O.P.) was a joint, $15 million venture by CBS and the Hollywood Turf Club. Intended to compete with Disneyland, California's then newest tourist attraction, P.O.P. extended along the beachfront for nearly half a mile. A labyrinth of arcades, curio shops, cafes, sideshows, and thrill rides, including a legendary roller coaster twisting above the sea, attracted over two million visitors the first year. But P.O.P. lacked the wit, charm, and sophistication of Disney's creation. After years of declining crowds, the controlling interests filed for bankruptcy in 1967. Abandoned and deteriorating, victimized by fire and neglect, the park was finally razed in 1975. Ocean Park reclaimed that stretch of beach for public use.

In the past decade Ocean Park has undergone a remarkable revitalization. A renaissance has emerged on Main Street, marking it as one of L.A.'s most fashionable commercial districts. Many older homes have been renovated, celebrating the architectural charm and merit of Ocean Park. Dozens of public wall murals have been painted, displaying a sense of place and identity.

Today, nestled against the gentle hillside crested by Fourth Street, Ocean Park is an alluring setting to walk and explore. This tour takes you to old piers, down narrow lanes, into small cafes, past sculpted gardens and Victorian cottages, before colorful wall murals, and along busy sidewalks of Main Street. As you walk in Ocean Park, savor the small town feeling of both its residents and its urban design.

OCEAN PARK WALK

1. Municipal Pier Carousel
2. Municipal Pier Fishing Area
3. The Promenade
4. Longevity Center
5. Gazebo
6. Murals
7. Wadsworth Avenue Sculptures
8. Victorian House
9. Horatio West Court
10. Townhouses
11. Housecourts
12. Mary Hotchkiss Park
13. Hollister Court
14. Mission Revival House
15. Spanish Colonial Revival House
16. Hansel and Gretel House
17. Craftsman Style House
18. Victorian House
19. Mural
20. Turning Point
21. Ocean Park Community Organization
22. Methodist Episcopal Church
23. Victorian House
24. Neo-Victorian Buildings
25. Mural
26. Ocean Park Branch Library
27. Merle Norman Building
28. Office Building
29. Mural
30. Acupressure Workshop
31. Napoleon French Pastry and Tearoom
32. Community Garden
33. World Gym
34. Dhaba Indian Restaurant
35. O'Mahoney Irish Whip
36. Pioneer Boulangerie
37. Santa Monica Civic Auditorium
38. Santa Monica City Hall
39. Rand Corporation
40. Main Street Freeway Bridge
41. Santa Monica Place

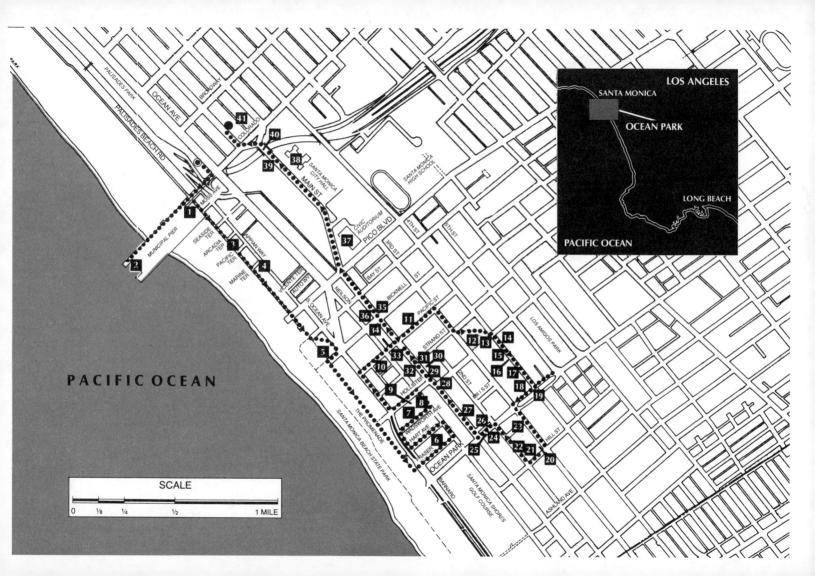

PACIFIC OCEAN

SCALE

0   ⅛   ¼   ½   1 MILE

LOS ANGELES

SANTA MONICA

OCEAN PARK

LONG BEACH

PACIFIC OCEAN

PARK

PALISADES PARK

OCEAN AVE

BROADWAY

PALISADES BEACH RD

COLORADO

MOSS AVE

MAIN ST

SANTA MONICA CITY HALL

SANTA MONICA HIGH SCHOOL

CIVIC AUDITORIUM

PICO BLVD

4TH ST

5TH ST

3RD ST

MUNICIPAL PIER

SEASIDE TER

ARCADIA TER

PACIFIC TER

APPIAN WAY

MARINE TER

VICENTE TER

AUTO WY

OCEAN AVE

NEILSON

BAY ST

BICKNELL

PACIFIC ST

STRAND ST

2ND ST

MILLS ST

LOS AMIGOS PARK

THE PROMENADE

SANTA MONICA BEACH STATE PARK

HOLLISTER

WADSWORTH AVE

HART AVE

FRASER

OCEAN PARK

BARNARD

SANTA MONICA SHORES GOLF COURSE

HILL ST

ASHLAND AVE

OCEAN PARK WALK

DIRECTIONS: *Take I-10 (Santa Monica Freeway) west and exit right on Fourth Street. After one block turn left on Colorado Avenue. Santa Monica Pier is at the foot of Colorado Avenue.*

PARKING: *Ample metered parking lines Ocean Avenue.*

PUBLIC
TRANSPORTATION: *RTD lines 4, 20, 22, 320.*
Santa Monica bus lines 1, 7, 10.

DISTANCE: *Less than three miles.*

DURATION: *An easy three-hour stroll including breakfast.*

SUGGESTED
ITINERARY: *Start at the Santa Monica Municipal Pier with a weekday breakfast at Cora's Coffee Shop at Ocean Avenue or a weekend breakfast at a cafe on the pier.*

SANTA MONICA MUNICIPAL PIER

The city's only remaining pier is actually two structures — the long and narrow Municipal Pier and the shorter but wider Newcomb Pier. Built between 1909 and 1921, the Municipal Pier was designed for a harbor master's office, commercial boat facilities, and public fishing areas.

Newcomb Pier was built as a privately owned amusement center in 1916. In its heyday it sustained a giant roller coaster, penny arcades, and the cavernous La Monica Ballroom, where 10,000 people could dance under an ornate Moorish roof to the swing music of the Big Bands.

The pier today is a playground to every type of urbanite. Its world famous carousel, arcades, seafood cafes, curio shops, and even a fortune teller entertain tourists and residents alike. Although the pier's end was severely damaged by winter storms in 1983, the city committed itself to restoring and improving the structure while retaining its funky, unpretentious character.

1. Municipal Pier Carousel (1922)

Paul Newman and Robert Redford filmed a chase scene here for ''The Sting,'' making this carousel world-famous. Built in 1922 and lovingly restored in 1981, this seaside merry-go-round is the only one remaining in a Los Angeles beach community. Its 1900 Wurlitzer organ, said to be the oldest in the country, whistles and whines toe-tapping melodies. For two bits (25¢), you can treat yourself to one of the true treasures of Southern California. After a ride, examine the photo exhibit detailing the painstaking process of restoration.

Constructed between 1916 and 1921, the Santa Monica Municipal Pier has been a favorite seaside landmark for its honky tonk cafes, arcades, carousel, and fishing area.

2. Municipal Pier Fishing Area

The end of the pier sustained severe damage from high tides and storm-thrashed waves in the winter of 1983. The harbor master's office, two cafes, and a historical photo exhibit collapsed into the sea. Yet fishermen continue to pack the end of the pier, as mackerel, bonita, halibut, rock cod and other sea life abound. Watch the pelicans swoop over the water and listen to the seals bark from the rock jetty. As you walk back, admire the spectacular view. To the northwest the Palisades fuse into the Santa Monica Mountains as the rugged Malibu coastline extends out to Point Dume. To the southeast the coastline forms a soft crescent, eventually jutting into the Pacific at the Palos Verdes Peninsula. Santa Monica Bay is breath-taking, especially after a storm or at sunset. The sleek new skyline of Santa Monica reflects the city's recent growth and redevelopment.

3. The Promenade

Extending between the Santa Monica and Venice piers, this walkway is the most popular pedestrian course in all of Los Angeles. Marking the edge of the city, the Promenade is bordered by dense cityscape on one side and wide, milk-white stretches of sand on the other. At one time, evening throngs dressed in formal attire strolled along the walk, reveling in the sunsets and in the public views. Now thousands of people from every walk of life ramble and roll, especially on beach-weather weekends.

Just south of the pier the famous Muscle Beach drew large crowds in the 1950's and '60's. Travel past the life guard headquarters, children's play areas, and Deco high-rises.

Interestingly, many of the older apartments and hotels once accommodated their more modest visitors by providing private beach access; tunnels traversed underneath sections of the Promenade so that beach-goers clad only in bathing suits would not be in the immediate public view of more formally attired strollers.

4. Longevity Center

1910 Ocean Front Walk

Nathan Pritikin's best-selling book *Live Longer Now* has proven so successful that he has set up this extensive nutritional center, which includes a staff of 200 nutritionists, physiologists, and psychologists. In the 1920's the Del Mar Beach Club occupied this elegant brick structure. The ill-fated Synanon Foundation, a drug rehabilitation community, established its headquarters here in the 1970's.

5. Gazebo

S. Ocean Avenue and Bicknell Street

At the picnic lawn area and colonnade, follow the stairs up to South Ocean Avenue. Rest awhile in this graceful gazebo and enjoy the cool breeze and ocean view.

BEACH COTTAGES
bounded by Barnard Way, Ocean Park Boulevard, Neilson Way, and Hollister Avenue

A nearly intact turn-of-the-century neighborhood, this four-block area contains some of the finest beach cottages in Santa Monica. When Ocean Park reached its heyday in the early 1900's, the blocks between the Promenade and Main

Street were densely developed with housing. Mission Revival, late Victorian, and Craftsman Style houses were stacked against one another along the narrow streets.

From 1930 to 1950 these neighborhoods experienced tremendous transition. Many of the residences became rundown and neglected. In 1958 the area barely escaped demolition by the Redevelopment Agency, which succeeded in destroying nearly a dozen similar blocks between Ocean Park Boulevard and Marine Street.

Fortunately, during the past decade this neighborhood has undergone a remarkable transformation. Residents have renovated and repainted many of the cottages. Shade trees have been planted to line the streets. Although speculation and inflation have painfully increased housing costs, nevertheless, the architectural charm is again being celebrated.

As you walk, notice the stylistic detail of the cottages: rusty weather vanes, ornate scroll work, decoratively carved wood beams, wind-worn brick chimneys, broad verandas, clattering wind chimes, and porch swings accent many of the residences.

These turn-of-the-century beach cottages on Wadsworth Avenue represent a delightful mix of architectural styles and detailing.

6. Murals

between Ocean Park Boulevard and Hart Street
Bold, graphic paintings adorn walls and garages. Below are listed four murals, some of which are sadly in disrepair:

"Rosie" by Art Mortimer (1971), 119 Ocean Park
  Boulevard
"Lynn Carey" by Art Mortimer (1978), Barnard Way near
  Ocean Park Boulevard
Faniciful portraits of women, anonymous, 132–138 Fraser
  Avenue
Untitled by Art Mortimer (1972), 161 Hart Street

7. Wadsworth Avenue Sculptures

between Barnard Way and Neilson Way
A modern embodiment of the Craftsman spirit finds expression in the dozen or so abstract sculptures which grace the front porches of many houses along Wadsworth Avenue. Designed by artist John N. Howard in the spring of 1982, the sculptures were shown that summer in the Oranges/Sardines Gallery in downtown Los Angeles. When Howard brought his artwork home to his Wadsworth Avenue flat, various admiring neighbors asked if they could display them on their front porches. Howard heartily complied and as a result, the abstract bric-a-brac sculptures create a startling yet complimentary mix of styles with the houses in this neighborhood.

8. House (ca. 1910)

151 Wadsworth Avenue
Among these residences, number 151 is unquestionably the grande dame. Its towering front cupola, steep corniced roof, elaborately hewn beams, and deep veranda all form a magnificent portrait of Victorian beachfront elegance.

9. Horatio West Court (1919)

140 Hollister Avenue
Designed by renowned California architect Irving Gill, these apartments dramatically broke with traditional styles of the early 1900's. The simple, uncluttered lines and surfaces previewed the Modern and International styles. Recently renovated, the court was declared an official Santa Monica landmark in 1979.

PACIFIC STREET
between South Ocean Avenue and Third Street

These four short blocks represent a cross section of Ocean Park's architecture over the last ninety years. Turn-of-the-century seafront shanties, '20's Craftsman Style bungalows, '30's Spanish Revival housecourts, '50's duplexes, and '80's high-tech, industrial condos all combine to create a high-density, well-integrated cityscape.

10. Townhouses (1982)

116–118½ Pacific Street
Innovative, austere, yet comfortably secure in design, these four two-story townhouses mix motifs from Deco, high-tech, Post-modern, and minimalist styles.

11. Housecourts

211–217 and 237 Pacific Street
Simple Colonial Revival and Craftsman Style courts.

FOURTH STREET
between Strand Street and Ocean Park Boulevard

Cresting the bluffs which gently rise above Ocean Park, Fourth Street offers grand views of Santa Monica Bay. During the past century many large homes have been built along it. Today, lined with Australian bottlebrush trees, Fourth Street reflects the stylistic diversity of L.A.'s architecture.

12. Mary Hotchkiss Park
Strand Street and Fourth Street
Overlooking the village of Ocean Park and the Pacific, gently terraced with wide lawns and inviting stairs, and shaded with ficus, palms, and pines, this green space provides a restful setting for nearby residents to sit, sun, chat, read, and write.

13. Hollister Court
2402 Fourth Street
These individual Craftsman Style bungalows, surrounding a lushly landscaped central walkway, were built in the 1910's.

14. House
2407 Fourth Street
Mission Revival, resembling a castle with its turreted tower and scalloped parapet.

15. House
2412 Fourth Street
Spanish Colonial Revival, accented with adobe tiles and spindled balconies.

16. House
2418 Fourth Street
Hansel and Gretel, complete with variegated shingles.

17. House
2424 Fourth Street
California Craftsman house built in 1911, declared an official city landmark in 1981 and restored in 1982; perhaps the most splendid example in Ocean Park.

18. House
2506 Fourth Street
Late Victorian house with Craftsman housecourt addition.

Austere Post-modern condominiums at 116 Pacific Avenue attest to Ocean Park's penchant for architectural innovation.

19. Ocean Park Underpass Mural

Ocean Park Boulevard and Fourth Street

Depicting the colorful history of Santa Monica, street muralists have transformed a monolithic concrete wall into the community's self-portrait. One side, by Jane Golden and associates, traces the area's evolving cityscape over the past century. The other, by Daniel Alonzo, depicts the sea life of whales and dolphins.

20. Turning Point

245 Hill Street

Based in an old house which originally belonged to Santa Monica's first fire chief, this agency provides emergency food and shelter assistance, counseling, and social service advocacy to many of Ocean Park's poorer residents.

21. Ocean Park Community Organization

235 Hill Street

Created and staffed by Ocean Park residents, OPCO is a neighborhood activist organization, serving the educational, environmental, commercial, and political needs of the community.

22. Methodist Episcopal Church (1875–76)

2621 Second Street

Built in 1875, later moved to this location, this was the first church structure in Santa Monica, and is probably the oldest wood frame building in the city. It was designated an official city landmark in 1977, and a local artist currently uses the structure as a private studio.

23. House (1885)

237 Beach Street

This Victorian farmhouse may be the oldest existing frame residence in Santa Monica. Currently being renovated by Tony Haig, the house was originally situated one-half block south, on Second Street. The steep-roofed house across the street (242 Beach Street) once served as the farm's carriage and milk barn.

24. Condominiums and Offices (1982)

2622 and 2628 Second Street

Whimsical hand crafted designs, reflecting L.A.'s stylistic playfulness, create an island of Neo-Victoriana in Ocean Park.

MAIN STREET
between Ocean Park Boulevard and Pico Boulevard

While Main Street southeast of Ocean Park Boulevard (see West Venice Walk) is best known for its ultra-chic eateries and boutiques, this area still projects a sense of a small town. Local residents frequent its cafes, markets, and shops. But far from being a bland "Anytown USA", these neighborhood businesses cater to an eclectic and eccentric local clientele. A weightlifting club faces a mom-and-pop grocery store; an acupressure clinic adjoins a hair salon; an aerobic dance studio borders an auto repair shop. Such a diverse setting creates an exciting place to explore, and deserves the name "Main Street."

25. **Mural: "The Old Ocean Park Pier"** (1975)

Ocean Park at Main Street

A collage of faceless merrymakers romps at Ocean Park's original seaside carnival, painted by Jane Golden and the Citywide Murals Project.

26. **Ocean Park Branch Library** (1917)

2601 Main Street

The oldest surviving library structure in Santa Monica. Inside this small yet elegant building are extensive community bulletin boards and books on local history. In 1977 it was declared an official city landmark.

27. **Merle Norman Building** (1935–36)

2525 Main Street

This wonderful Streamlined Moderne structure once served as the headquarters for Merle Norman Cosmetics. Note its chrome strips and geometric Indian motifs.

28. **Office Building**

2401 Main Street

Behind the colorful glass bottle door is a delightful stained glass cupola above a winding staircase.

29. **Mural**

2339 Main Street at Hollister Avenue

An exotic landscape of forested mountains, swaying palms, and a tropical lagoon entertains passersby in this street rendering by Mike Caple.

30. **Acupressure Workshop**

2307 Main Street

New Age consciousness serves the community in this esoteric health practice, where acupressure, herbal medicine, shiatsu massage, and self-healing arts are taught.

31. **Napoleon French Pastry and Tearoom**

2301 Main Street

A charming neighborhood cafe specializing in country French pastries, quiches, and cappuccino. Sit awhile, sample the fare, and observe the variety of locals.

32. **Community Garden**

Main Street and Strand Street

Sunflowers, artichokes, and sweet peas thrive in this neighborhood garden, which is owned, planned, and parceled by the city of Santa Monica. Local renters may grow their own gardens here, creating greenery and breathing space. You are welcome to admire the flowers and vegetables, but please do not trespass on garden plots.

33. **World Gym**

2210 Main Street

The musty smell of gym sweat and the clanking of heavy weights greet the street. Walk upstairs for a peek at this legendary gym and its bodybuilders.

34. **Dhaba Indian Restaurant**

2104 Main Street

Exotic East Indian cuisine, outdoor patio dining, and sitar music, all at a moderate price. Dinner only.

35. **O'Mahoney Irish Whip**

2029 Main Street

Across from a Basque bakery and an Indian restaurant, this Irish pub adds to the cosmopolitan character of Ocean Park.

36. Pioneer Boulangerie
2012 Main Street

An outdoor patio and an indoor buffet serve fresh baked
pastries and breads, soups, salads, and other light fare. The
upstairs dining room prepares family style Basque dinners.
Wander around the gourmet nooks and wine-filled crannies or
watch jacobread being baked in the original Pyrenees brick
ovens. Boulangerie deserves a civic award for providing a
''gift to the street'' in its beautifully landscaped and well
maintained grounds!

SANTA MONICA CIVIC CENTER
Main Street between Pico Boulevard and Colorado Avenue

Until the late 1930's, this area served as a terminus for
the Santa Fe Railroad. The city purchased the land, tore up
the tracks, and designated the area as the center for Santa
Monica's government. Today broad lawns, shade trees, and
parking lots offer breathing space between both civic and
private structures which rise above Main Street.

37. Santa Monica Civic Auditorium (1956)
1855 Main Street

Seating 3,500 people, this auditorium hosts jazz and rock
concerts, trade exhibitions, and other shows. For a brief

*Santa Monica Place, a three-level skylit galleria designed by Frank Gehry
in 1980, is an exciting people-oriented center which has won many
architectural awards.*

period in the 1960's, the annual Academy Awards ceremonies spotlighted Hollywood's greats in this hall.

38. Santa Monica City Hall (1938)
1685 Main Street

Designed by Donald B. Parkinson and J. M. Estep, this Classical Moderne structure with its elaborate mosaic tile entrance was declared an official landmark in 1979. The main lobby murals illustrate Santa Monica's ''good life'' in the 1930's and follow the city's history.

39. Rand Corporation
1700 Main Street

Self-defined as ''a private, nonprofit institution engaged in research and analysis of matters affecting national security and the public welfare and in the operation of education programs,'' this organization produces research which is often quoted in both government and private journals.

40. Main Street Freeway Bridge
From the vantage point of this overpass, the twisting freeway and its currents of traffic resemble a river. Once Olympic Boulevard passed beneath this bridge and emptied through the tunnel, both of which were built in the 1930's.

41. Santa Monica Place (1980)
bounded by Colorado Avenue, Broadway, Second and Fourth Streets

Designed by Frank Gehry and Associates, this three-level, skylit galleria creates an unconventional and alluring setting for 150 shops and two major department stores. In Gehry's words, ''This project was an opportunity to create a major public space in downtown Santa Monica and make an architectural statement which could, conceivably, set the pace for future development.'' Gehry's design succeeds in creating such a place. Major entrances present dramatic and inviting post-modern spaces. Fountains, pools, tree-lined terraces, tiered levels, and bold angles all contribute to create an exciting people-oriented center.

For Further Reading on Ocean Park:

See Santa Monica bibliography.

VENICE WALKS

Venice today might be compared to Central-Park-at-the-Beach or a circus on wheels. On any warm beach-weather weekend, tens of thousands of Angelenos flock to the wide sandy beach and the carnival-like Ocean Front Walk. Roller-skaters, street musicians, artisans, and urbanites of every color parade along the seafront walk.

Yet Venice caters to more than just the idiosyncracies of beach people. Along Main Street with its swank cafes and chic boutiques, affluent shoppers and sophisticates stroll. Contrasting with the festive spontaneity of Ocean Front Walk, Main Street tends to be stylishly urbane.

And just inland another Venetian community celebrates its unique character. Two miles of shallow canals still exist, with Craftsman Style bungalows and Post-modern monuments nestled alongside the waterways. Ducks and geese paddle beneath lacy footbridges. Some waterfront homes even have miniature docks and canoes, adding to the picturesque setting.

With its diverse communities and unique urban design, Venice today owes its existence largely to one man — Abbot Kinney. The wealthy magnate and manufacturer of Sweet Caporal cigarettes, Kinney had been involved in many coastal ventures before he built Venice in 1904. An amateur horticulturalist, he began the nation's first experimental forestry station in Rustic Canyon in 1887. About that time he joined with Francis Ryan and A. R. Fraser to develop the seaside resort village of Ocean Park. Their corporation owned nearly all of the land between present-day Pico Boulevard and Marina del Rey.

Kinney, however, had more imaginative and daring dreams. As a world traveler, he had visited Europe several times. Impressed with the cultural vitality of the opera houses, art museums, concert halls, and urban promenades, Kinney became an enthusiast and connoisseur of the arts. He made up his mind that Los Angeles, with its Mediterranean climate, diverse geography, and almost limitless potential for growth was the ideal region for an artistic community which would spark a cultural renaissance in California.

Inspired by the romantic beauty of Venice, Italy, Kinney envisioned a California seaside city interlaced with canals and footpaths. Italian villas and Byzantine hotels would welcome artisans and craftspeople from around the country; auditoriums would present the best and brightest musicians and lecturers. Kinney imagined a Venice of America where Los Angeles would lead the world in cultural vitality.

Deciding to leave the Ocean Park partnership, Kinney acquired the undeveloped seafront property south of Rose Avenue. Only a few houses dotted the sandy dunes. Numerous hollows and marshes filled much of the land, forming an estuary where Ballona Creek met the ocean. Hunters and fishermen had frequented these wetlands for years.

In the summer of 1904, men, horses, and steam shovels began to dredge the Grand Canal. Two networks of smaller canals branched from this major waterway. A central lagoon was created; from here a wide street led to the ocean. Two large pipes under this road, called Windward Avenue, would allow the lagoon and the canals to be flushed each day by the ocean tides. Walkstreets were planned in the beachfront section and tunnels were built under Ocean Front Walk to allow hotel guests unhindered access to the beach. A huge pier was constructed at the foot of Windward Avenue, complete with cafes and a 3,600 seat auditorium.

Despite construction problems due to harsh winter weather, Venice of America prepared to welcome its first guests by the summer. On June 30, 1905, Kinney opened the tunnel gates under Windward Avenue; by nightfall eight miles of canals were filled with water. On July 4, a grand celebration welcomed over 40,000 visitors who marveled at Kinney's new town. Elaborate Italian Renaissance hotels and arched colonnades lined Windward. Over 17,000 electric lights sparkled along the canals and footpaths as fireworks and band concerts greeted the crowds. During the summer Kinney brought many leading artists and writers to his cultural oasis, including author Helen Hunt Jackson, actress Sarah Bernhardt, and the Chicago Symphony.

But the public did not share Kinney's cultural interests. Concerts and plays were only lightly attended. Instead, the day visitors and weekend guests flocked to the few thrill rides and sideshows. The artful entrepreneur decided to follow the public's lead; soon the promenades and pier took on a honky-tonk atmosphere. Roller coasters, casinos, parades, innumerable concessionaires, and a huge bathhouse thrilled the visitors.

From 1910 to 1920 Venice celebrated its heyday. Thousands rode the interurban trolleys to the beachfront every weekend. Many others bought small lots and built cottages along the romantic canals. A number of silent film stars owned weekend retreats in Venice, including Clara Bow, Mary Pickford, Rudolf Valentino, Fatty Arbuckle, and Charlie Chaplin.

But problems began to emerge. The extensive networks of canals had been poorly engineered. With only one primary outlet, the waterways were often dirty and stagnant. The sewer system was inadequate for the growing town. With shifting ocean currents and winter storms, beach erosion was a problem, creating costly repair work. And the narrow streets and bridges, designed primarily for pedestrians, were unable to handle the increasing needs of automobile traffic and parking.

The decline of Venice began in 1920 with Abbot Kinney's death. Disaster soon followed when a fire destroyed the Venice Pier, and months later a few city officials were found guilty of embezzling city monies, weakening public confidence. And with Prohibition the city's tax base eroded as liquor taxes and licenses were outlawed. Interestingly, though, speakeasies soon operated underneath Windward Avenue in the hotel basements and tunnels.

In 1925 Venice residents voted to be annexed by Los Angeles. Without warning, Los Angeles enforced its "Blue Laws" over the newly acquired territory. Gambling, public dancing, and business hours were severely restricted.

Debate raged over the future of the canals; a strong contingent of residents pressed to have the waterways filled in and paved over to accommodate automobiles, and the city did not want to maintain and repair the canals. Despite opposition, primarily from property owners unwilling to be assessed for the costs, in 1929 the canals in northern Venice were filled in. The crowds declined, and during the Depression, most of the amusement piers were dismantled. Over the next forty years Venice became a nearly forgotten corner of L.A., attracting Beatniks in the late 1950's and hippies and flower children in the late '60's.

In the early 1970's, the public began to notice Venice once more. The district had become synonymous with an eccentric and casual lifestyle, epitomizing California's image as the edge of the continent where "anything goes." Ocean Front Walk began to attract thousands of weekend visitors. Murals appeared throughout the city. Venice once again became the most popular pedestrian course in Los Angeles.

With all the changes, Venice still celebrates its original character. In the last decade many old structures have been renovated to reflect Kinney's imaginative designs. Art galleries and fine cafes have opened in old brick buildings. New structures by such architects as Frank O. Gehry, Frederick Fisher, and Thane Roberts reflect the latest innovative styles. Thousands of people continue to parade along Ocean Front Walk on weekends. Kinney's dream is alive today: Venice gives Angelenos a place to play, promenade, and people watch.

The first walk in this chapter is designed to introduce you to both the cityscape and the people in northern Venice. And because Venice is still a bohemian refuge, the walk leads to many of the watering holes which poets, writers, and artists visit. As you walk this tour, keep an eye open for places where you would like to spend more time later, particularly along Main Street.

The second walk leads to the best that remains of Kinney's fantasy. You will encounter Windward Avenue's arched colonnades and Venice's only remaining canals. The tour also leads to the edge of L.A.'s newest waterfront fantasy — Marina del Rey, the world's largest manmade small-craft harbor. Finally, you explore East Ocean Front Walk, where honky-tonk and avant garde collide. Here fishing piers and art galleries, corndog stands and nouvelle cuisine cafes, roller skaters and radicals mix.

1. Venice Post Office
2. Windward Farms
3. Aaardvark's
4. Venice Arcades
5. Mural
6. Venice Pavilion
7. Mural
8. Mural
9. Sidewalk Cafe
10. Small World Books
11. Lafayette Coffee Shop
12. Venice Bathhouse
13. Park Avenue and Thornton Avenue
14. Housecourt
15. Bay Cities Synagogue
16. Figtree's Cafe
17. Ocean View Hotel
18. Path to Main Street
19. Methodist Episcopal Church
20. Victorian Houses
21. Neo-Victorian Condos and Offices
22. Murals
23. Mural
24. Heritage Square Museum
25. The Chronicle Restaurant
26. Jadis
27. Merlin McFly Magical Bar and Grill
28. Omelette Parlor
29. Wildflour Pizza
30. Colors of the Wind
31. Bolen Gallery
32. The Buttery
33. Famous Enterprise Fish Co.
34. Charmers Market
35. Parkhurst Building
36. One Life Natural Foods
37. Meyera Restaurant
38. Via Dolce Confectioners
39. Rose Cafe
40. Gold's Gym
41. Pedestrian Subway
42. Paloma Avenue

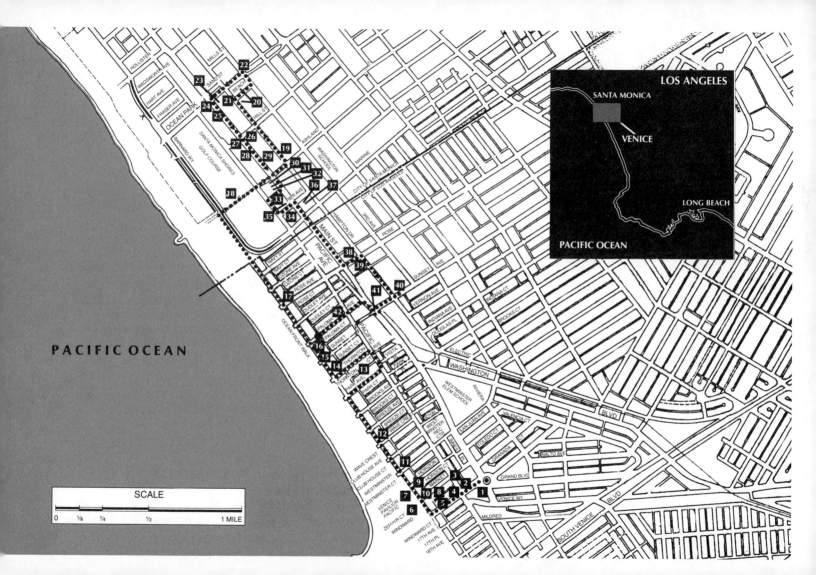

PACIFIC OCEAN

PACIFIC OCEAN

SCALE

0   1/8   1/4   1/2   1 MILE

LOS ANGELES

SANTA MONICA

VENICE

LONG BEACH

PACIFIC OCEAN

NORTH VENICE WALK

DIRECTIONS: *Take I-10 (Santa Monica Freeway) west, exit Fourth Street left (east). Turn right on Pico Boulevard, then left on Main Street and follow to Windward Avenue.*

Parking: *Unfortunately, parking is scarce, particularly on weekends. Plan to arrive by 9:30 a.m. and park near the traffic circle.*

PUBLIC TRANSPORTATION: *RTD line 33. Santa Monica bus line 1.*

DISTANCE: *A bit more than three miles.*

DURATION: *A leisurely three hours, plus extra time to browse in shops and cafes.*

SUGGESTED ITINERARY: *Start at Windward Avenue and Main Street, and stop for a 10 a.m. breakfast at either the Sidewalk Cafe or the Lafayette Coffee Shop. Conclude the tour with cafe latte or herbal tea at Figtree's.*

CLOTHES: *Light, casual wear for both beachfront walking and windowshopping.*

WINDWARD AVENUE
between the traffic circle and Ocean Front Walk

When Abbot Kinney first designed Venice in 1904, this area was the center of his romantic community. Kinney lined Windward Avenue with arched colonnades exhibiting the splendor of a Californian Byzantine design. All the canals led to the Grand Lagoon (now the traffic circle), where boating docks, aquatic activities, and a high dive provided recreation. A major Pacific Electric Railway line stopped at Windward and Pacific, bringing thousands of visitors from the hot inland valleys to the cool ocean breezes.

1. **Venice Post Office**
   southwest corner of Main Street and Windward Avenue
   Walk inside and examine Edward Biberton's 1932 mural depicting the iridescent history of early Venice. Kinney's dream evolves from placid canals, amusement parks, and gondola excursions to annexation by Los Angeles, oil wells, and canal fill-ins.

2. **Windward Farms**
   105 Windward Avenue
   A delightful array of farm fresh vegetables, fruits, juices, and sandwiches. An ideal place to pick up picnic snacks for the beach.

3. **Aaardvark's**
   156 Pacific Avenue
   Funky used clothes at cheap, cheap prices.

4. **Venice Arcades**
   Windward Avenue between Main Street and Ocean Front Walk

Only a few buildings remain of Kinney's original Venice.
These colonnades with their arched walkways and bas-reliefs
reflect an earlier era of romantic facades and images.

5. Mural: "St. Charles Painting"

25 Windward Avenue
Painted by Terry Schoonhoven in 1979, this trompe l'oeil
mural once created a startlingly realistic portrait of the
opposite cityscape. Sadly, the mural now suffers from neglect
and vandalism.

6. Venice Pavilion

Ocean Front Walk at Windward Avenue
Kinney planned Windward Avenue as the resort's major
commercial thoroughfare. Leading west from the Grand
Lagoon, Windward guided thousands of weekend revelers to
the sprawling old Venice Pier. There thrill rides, arcades,
bingo parlors, a concert hall, and the old Ship Cafe welcomed
the crowds. After declining revenues and a series of disastrous
fires, the pier was torn down in 1947. In the mid-1960's, the
present reinforced concrete structure was built, and it now
serves as a community recreation center, attracting picnickers,
disco-roller-skaters, and frisbee throwers. Many of the
pavilion's large concrete panels form a series of murals
depicting the history of Venice, painted in 1973 under the
direction of muralist Judy Baca. Over sixty local artists and
volunteers contributed long hours to this community art
project.

*A few of the original arched walkways and bas-relief decorated colonnades
built along Windward Avenue in 1904 continue to shade pedestrians.*

7. Mural: "Venice on the Half Shell"

Venice Pavilion facing Windward Avenue
Inspired by Botticelli's 1485 painting "The Birth of Venus," this superb surrealistic mural by R. Gronk portrays Venice of the 1980's.

8. Mural: "The Fall of Icarus"

Speedway between Windward Avenue and Market Street
A fading surrealistic portrait of Los Angeles by artist Terry Schoonhoven. L.A.'s scraggly natural landscape reclaims a deserted drive-in theater, as two nearly-fallen angels flit above a movie screen showing a lone astronaut in space.

9. Sidewalk Cafe

1401 Ocean Front Walk
Although the menu is mediocre and predictable, musicians, a full bar, and spectacular frontage along the Walk provide an exciting place to watch the circus parade by.

10. Small World Books and Art Gallery

1407 Ocean Front Walk
Browse through the voluminous display of magazines, local history books, and works by local writers and artists.

11. Lafayette Coffee Shop

1219 Ocean Front Walk
Although this modest cafe appears to be only a typical "greasy spoon" coffee shop, it is a favorite local landmark. Sit in Ruby's section and be charmed by her Southern amiability. A

wiry, tender, and street-wise Mississippian, Ruby has worked here for fourteen years. Calling herself the "Venice Mama" to countless regulars, she can tell you many stories about the hodgepodge of locals whose photographs are on the walls.

The Lafayette sits on the first floor of a white-glazed brick building which once presumed the name of the Waldorf Hotel. Built in 1914, it billed itself as "the only hotel in the world with bungalows on the roof." Regular guests in the 1920's included Charlie Chaplin and Clara Bow.

Entitled "Venice on the Half Shell," this surrealistic mural by R. Gronk at the Venice Pavilion was inspired by Botticelli's 1485 painting "The Birth of Venus."

12. The Venice Bathhouse (1983)

Breeze Avenue and Ocean Front Walk

Designed after the original bathhouse at Main Street and Windward Avenue, this new structure includes shops, cafes, offices, condos, and a three-story glass-roofed gallery.

13. Park Avenue and Thornton Avenue

between Ocean Front Walk and Pacific Avenue

These two footpaths capture much of the residential ambiance of early Venice. Between 1905 and 1925, hundreds of beach cottages were built between the Promenade and Main Street. Ranging from clapboard seafront shanties to elaborate Craftsman Style manors, the houses provided cool, restful refuge for Angelenos weary of the inland heat and dust. Below are a few historical notes on some of these homes, reflecting the early popularity of Venice for film stars and artists.

10 Park Avenue: Mary Pickford and Wallace Reed once owned beach houses on these empty lots.

16 Park Avenue: Originally this Norman cottage was owned by Thornton Kinney, the son of Venice's founder.

17 Park Avenue: Olivia de Havilland resided here in the 1930's.

39 Thornton Avenue: Silent screen star Fatty Arbuckle lived in this large Craftsman Style house in the 1920's.

18 Thornton Avenue: Neighbors say that in the late 1960's, a young actress named Jane Fonda lived here in the upstairs flat.

16 Thornton Avenue: This sandcastle-like apartment house once served as a prestigious hotel. Locals claim that Isadora Duncan lived here for several years in the 1920's, often performing modern dances on the roof at sunset. Sweet

William, the counterculture author of *Venice of America*, resided in the penthouse apartment in the 1970's.

14. Housecourt

517 Ocean Front Walk

This intriguing red brick, green tiled Mediterranean housecourt was once owned by Eddie Cantor.

15. Bay Cities Synagogue

505 Ocean Front Walk

A strong Jewish community has resided in Venice for decades. This temple serves many of the elderly Jews who were highlighted by anthropologist Barbara Myerhoff in her book and film *Number Our Days*.

16. Figtree's Cafe

429 Ocean Front Walk

This moderately priced, gourmet-minded health food cafe offers an atypical menu, including home baked pastries, espresso, stuffed potatoes, and manicotti. Emmy, the gracious hostess, will seat you inside (which resembles a Haight Street coffee house in San Francisco) or outside on the sunny patio, where you can watch the passing menagerie.

17. Ocean View Hotel

5 Rose Avenue

Now beautifully restored as a residence for senior citizens, this elegant hotel drew national attention on May 16, 1926. On that morning, evangelist Aimee Semple McPherson, the flamboyant founder of the Four Square Church, left her suite in the Ocean View Hotel and walked to the sea with her secretary for a swim. Sister Aimee waded into the surf and disappeared. Within hours thousands of her followers gathered at the beach, to pray and conduct a desperate search for her body. One lifeguard drowned in the futile search, and a mourner committed suicide. After a month of no leads, she was presumed dead and a memorial service was held in Venice. But on June 23, a weary Sister Aimee reappeared near Douglas, Arizona, claiming to have escaped from kidnappers. She was welcomed to Los Angeles by 100,000 joyous followers, but later contradictions in her testimony created a scandal over her credibility.

18. Path to Main Street

Redevelopment has demolished old amusement piers and Craftsman Style beach cottages in order to construct parking lots and high-rises. Fortunately, developments like Sea Colony display a sense of intimacy in urban planning and design. This new walkway at the traffic signal gracefully curves to Ashland Avenue and Main Street.

SECOND STREET
between Ashland Avenue and Ocean Park Boulevard

Paralleling the razzmatazz of Main Street, Second Street evokes a sense of calm and quiet. Craftsman Style bungalows, Spanish Revival cottages, and a few Victorians made this section architecturally interesting.
and a few Victorians made this section architecturally interesting.

19. Methodist Episcopal Church (1875)

2621 Second Street
Built in 1875, later moved to this site, this was the first church structure in Santa Monica and is probably the oldest wood frame building in the town. It was designated an official Santa Monica landmark in 1977, and a local artist now uses it as a private studio.

20. House (1885)

237 Beach Street
This Victorian farmhouse may be the oldest existing frame residence in Santa Monica. Currently being renovated by Tony Haig, the house was originally situated one-half block south, on Second Street. The steep-roofed house across the street (242 Beach Street) once served as the farm's carriage and milk barn.

21. Condominiums and Offices

2622 and 2628 Second Street
Whimsical hand crafted designs, reflecting L.A.'s stylistic playfulness, create an island of Neo-Victoriana in Ocean Park.

22. Ocean Park Underpass Murals

Ocean Park and Fourth Street
Depicting the colorful history of Santa Monica, street muralists have transformed monolithic concrete walls into a community's self portrait. One side, by Jane Golden and associates, traces the area's evolving cityscape over the past century. The other, by Daniel Alonzo, celebrates the sea life of whales and dolphins.

23. Mural: "The Old Ocean Park Pier"

Ocean Park Boulevard at Main Street
A collage of faceless merrymakers romps at Ocean Park's original seaside carnival, painted in 1975 by Jane Golden and the Citywide Murals Project.

MAIN STREET
between Ocean Park Boulevard and Rose Avenue

Ten years ago Main Street was lackluster; clapboard storefronts and family owned businesses served a quiet working class neighborhood. But during the past decade, speculators and developers have renovated the architectural charm and commercial focus of the area.

Lined with art galleries, gourmet cafes, antique stores, New Age bookshops, and trendy clothing boutiques, Main Street resembles San Francisco's Union Street or New York City's SoHo. Westside wealthy and South Bay singles, Venetian literati and Santa Monica glitterati stroll along its sidewalks.

Listed below are a few of the scores of stores to explore. Take time to examine the menus and rear patios of restaurants, some of which are quite innovatively designed.

24. Heritage Square Museum
2612 Main Street

Originally designed for the son of Santa Monica's founder by architect Sumner P. Hunt, this Colonial Revival house was built in 1894 and moved to its present location in 1977. Local history enthusiasts have volunteered long hours towards restoring the Victorian character of the rooms with period furnishings. Browse in the excellent museum bookstore, admire the historical exhibits, and enjoy the interior displays.

Ocean Front Walk on a "beach weather" weekend attracts crowds of eccentric Angelenos, many of whom can't seem to give up their wheels, whatever the setting.

25. The Chronicle Restaurant
2640 Main Street

Lodged in a restored late Victorian house built in 1906, this expensive restaurant serves superb food amidst the charm of Victorian decor.

26. Jadis
2701 Main Street

Art nouveau, deco, and moderne clothing, accessories, and furniture, all hand selected and impeccable in quality and taste.

27. Merlin McFly Magical Bar and Grill

2702 Main Street

A busy neighborhood pub, stuffed with Victoriana. Portraits of legendary magicians from ages past are etched and colored on huge stained glass windows. The hand carved, dragon-headed mahogany bar belches smoke and delights the eye. Order a drink, sit awhile, and enjoy the ambiance.

28. Omelette Parlor

2732 Main Street

Enjoy eggceptionally hearty breakfasts: fluffy omelettes, home baked breads, and fresh fruit. A fascinating collage of historical photos on the walls spotlights the past century in Ocean Park.

29. Wildflour Pizza

2807 Main Street

Superb Boston-style thin crust pizza, judged as L.A.'s best by the *Los Angeles Times*.

30. Colors of the Wind

2900 Main Street

Kites and pennants of every imagination! An exciting store to explore, filled with wonderful ideas for celebrating the wind.

31. Bolen Gallery

2904 Main Street

Original paintings, serigraphs, and sculptures, often by renowned artists.

32. The Buttery

2906 Main Street

Flaky croissants, fresh baked blueberry muffins, and a host of other mouth-watering pastries waft delicious scents and temptations.

33. Famous Enterprise Fish Co.

174 Kinney Street

Ocean fresh seafood, charcoal-broiled and mesquite-smoked behind an intriguing glass-walled cooking area. The lounge and oyster bar offer an intimate and relaxing place for a late afternoon chat with a good friend.

34. Charmers Market

175 Marine Street

Charmers has transformed an old bank into a treasure house of delectables, a palatable palace of gourmet delights. Soft lighting, new wave music, a canopied continental cafe, and an espresso bar provide a centerpiece for an epicurean marketplace. The fruit seems hand polished, the wine stacked in the vault is hand selected, and the pastries are hand prepared. Wander around and appreciate this sumptuous tribute to hedonistic delights.

35. Parkhurst Building

2942 Main Street

A marvelous Spanish Revival structure with intricately patterned brickwork. Built in 1922 originally as a Van de Kamp's bakery, this building contrasts beautifully with the nearby Sea Colony condos.

36. One Life Natural Foods

3001 Main Street

Organic fruits and vegetables, 335 kinds of herbs, whole grain breads, and a plethora of other natural foods are offered to eclectic, health-minded shoppers.

37. Meyera Restaurant

3009 Main Street
An exotic wedding of French and vegetarian cuisines.
Innovative hors d'oeuvres, creative entrees, and novel desserts
make a later visit for dinner worthwhile.

38. Via Dolce Confectioners

215 Rose Avenue
The buzzing, brilliantly colored neon menu emblazons a
tantalizing list of Venetian liqueur ice creams. Sample the
chocolate raspberry truffle, the creme de menthe, or the
Kahlua. Chocolate liqueur truffles complement the luscious
specialties.

39. Rose Cafe

220 Rose Avenue
A popular neighborhood bistro, the Rose offers a variety of
settings and menus. Once a 1930's gas company dispatch
office, the Rose has transformed the structure into two outdoor
patios, two indoor dining areas, an emporium selling culinary
accessories, and an extensive display area for its own bakery
and gourmet deli. Soft jazz and classical music contribute to
an ambiance of casual, unhurried dining among an often
mosaic crowd. The high-tech design is complemented by
works of local artists.

40. Gold's Gym

364 Hampton Drive
Walk inside this legendary mecca for bodybuilders and admire
the serious-minded men and women as they strain at their
workouts. The clunks and clanks of the weights mix with the
grunts and heaves of the lifters as they toil for physical
perfection.

41. Pedestrian Subway

Main Street and Sunset Avenue
Originially designed in the '20's to allow pedestrian access
beneath the Pacific Electric Railroad tracks, these subways are
scattered throughout the older areas of Los Angeles.

42. Paloma Avenue

between Pacific Avenue and Ocean Front Walk
Return to the boardwalk via this serene footpath. Note the
fascinating collection of architectural styles, from Craftsman
Style bungalows to pre–World War I brick apartments to
Post-modern corrugated metal structures. Conclude your walk
by resting at Figtree's Cafe.

SOUTH VENICE WALK

1. Traffic Circle
2. Venice Post Office
3. Pelican's Catch Restaurant
4. Eighteenth Street
5. Canal Street
6. Craftsman Style Apartments
7. Bungalow Courts
8. Venice Boulevard
9. Mural
10. English Cottage
11. Neo-Victorian House
12. Grand Canal
13. Venice Canals Children's Park
14. Post-modern House
15. Post-modern House
16. Bungalow Court
17. Baja Cantina and Siamese Gardens
18. Washington Street Commercial District
19. Beach House
20. Venice Fishing Pier
21. West Beach Cafe
22. L.A. Louver Gallery

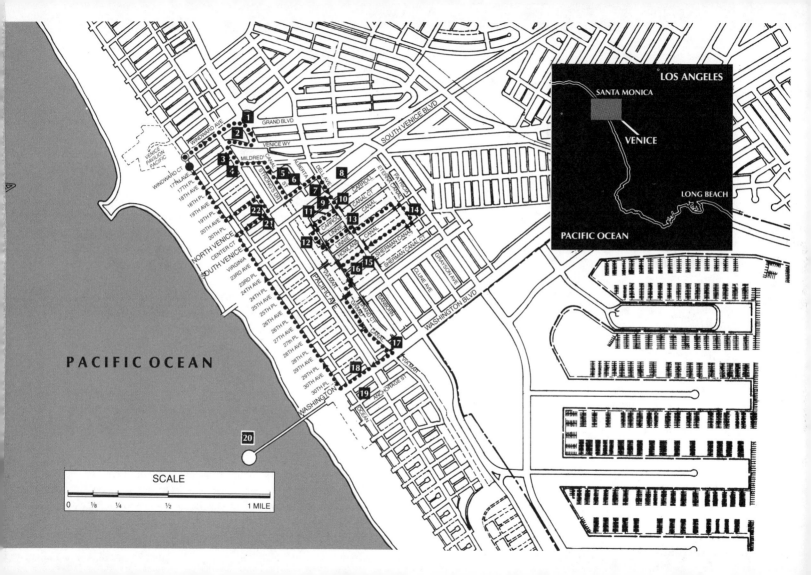

PACIFIC OCEAN

PACIFIC OCEAN

LOS ANGELES

SANTA MONICA

VENICE

LONG BEACH

PACIFIC OCEAN

SCALE

0   1/8   1/4   1/2   1 MILE

GRAND BLVD

VENICE WY

SOUTH VENICE BLVD

WINDWARD AVE

VENICE PAVILION PACIFIC

WINDWARD CT

17TH AVE
17TH PL
18TH AVE
18TH PL
19TH AVE
19TH PL
20TH AVE
20TH PL
CENTER CT

NORTH VENICE
SOUTH VENICE

VIRGINIA
23RD AVE
23RD PL
24TH AVE
24TH PL
25TH AVE
25TH PL
26TH AVE
26TH PL
27TH AVE
27TH PL
28TH AVE
28TH PL
29TH AVE
29TH PL
30TH AVE
30TH PL

WASHINGTON

MILDRED CANAL

STRONG DR

ALBERTA ST

DEL AVE

CARROLL

LINNIE

HOWLAND

CABRILLO

CANAL

CANAL CT

CARROLL CANAL

LINNIE CANAL

HOWLAND CANAL

SHERMAN CANAL

SHERMAN CANAL CT

EL TERRE DR

PATRICK

STRONG DR

VIA MARINA

GRAND CANAL

SANBORN

CLUNE AVE

GRAYSON AVE

WASHINGTON BLVD

OCEAN

ANCHORAGE ST

VIA MARINA

1
2
3
4
5
6
7
8
9
10
11
12
13
14
15
16
17
18
19
20
21
22

SOUTH VENICE WALK

DIRECTIONS: *Take I-10 (Santa Monica Freeway) west, exit Fourth Street left (east). Turn right on Pico Boulevard, then left on Main Street and follow to Windward Avenue.*

Parking: *Unfortunately, parking is scarce, particularly on weekends. Plan to arrive by 9:30 a.m. and park near the traffic circle.*

PUBLIC
TRANSPORTATION *RTD line 33.*
Santa Monica bus line 1.

CLOTHES: *Light, casual wear for both beachfront walking and windowshopping.*

DISTANCE: *Less than two and a half miles.*

DURATION: *A relaxing three hour exploration.*

SUGGESTED
ITINERARY: *Start at Windward Avenue and Ocean Front Walk, and have a 9:30 a.m. breakfast at the Sidewalk Cafe, 1401 Ocean Front Walk. On the tour, stop at John's Market and buy some bread to feed the ducks in the canals.*

WINDWARD AVENUE: KINNEY'S HEART OF VENICE

When Kinney first designed Venice around a network of placid canals and walkstreets in 1904, Windward Avenue served as the community's heart. Lined with elaborate Byzantine and Renaissance style buildings, Windward's shaded colonnades led from the central Grand Lagoon to the old Venice Pier. The St. Mark's Hotel on Windward Avenue and Ocean Front Walk hosted many celebrities, including Mary Pickford, Buster Keaton, and Sarah Bernhardt. Genteel crowds strolled along the avenues, canals, and walks.

Even though the area has undergone tremendous transition during the past half-century, you can still discover glimpses of the original Venice. Observe the ornate colonnades, detailed bas-reliefs, and old brick walls. Imagine how Venice must have appeared in its halcyon years. And notice the new spirit of life: cafes, galleries, murals, funky boutiques, and renovated buildings abound.

1. **Traffic Circle**
   Windward Avenue and Main Street
   At this site sixty years ago, the Grand Lagoon provided an arena for aquatic events and activities. From its expanse the canals branched to create a web of waterways. In 1928, tons of dirt fill formed this traffic circle.

2. **Venice Post Office**
   southwest corner of Main Street and Windward Avenue
   Originally on this site a Craftsman Style viewing pavilion overlooked the Grand Lagoon. In 1913 a huge roller coaster,

Tom Prior's "Race Through the Clouds," zoomed riders overhead. When the traffic circle was created, the present structure was built. Walk inside and view artist Edward Biberton's mural depicting the first thirty years of Venice's history.

3. Pelican's Catch Restaurant
1715 Pacific Avenue
A moderately priced seafood cafe, offering ocean-fresh fare.

4. Eighteenth Street
between Pacific Street and Ocean Front Walk
One of the few brick-paved streets in Los Angeles. One wonders how this lane escaped an assault of asphalt.

5. Canal Street
between Mildred Avenue and North Venice Boulevard
Once an extension of the Grand Canal to the Grand Lagoon, beneath the pavement and dirt fill rests one of Kinney's first canals, a portion of which may be seen from the edge of N. Venice Boulevard.

6. Craftsman Style Apartment Building
209 North Venice Boulevard
A grand example of Craftsman Style architecture: heavy wooden beams, shingled sides, wide eaves, wooden interiors, and leaded cut-glass windows exemplify the beauty of this design.

7. Bungalow Courts
Dell Avenue and North Venice Boulevard
Simple one-story courts hug each corner. Originally built between 1910 and 1920 as vacation rentals, the bungalows are now rented as permanent apartments.

8. Venice Boulevard Parkway
Dusty and weed-strewn, this island once cradled Venice's major Pacific Electric rail line to downtown Los Angeles.

VENICE CANAL NEIGHBORHOOD

In 1929 all but three miles of Venice's canals were filled in and paved over. Fortunately, these waterways escaped the steamshovel and bulldozer. At the time, this area was only partially developed and the residents were unable to afford the city assessment for fill-in costs.

As Venice declined in the 1930's and '40's, this neighborhood became tumble-down and neglected.

By the late 1960's the canals had deteriorated into stagnant, murky pools. But because of its isolation, uniqueness, and cheap rent, the neighborhood became a haven for hippies and other counterculture enthusiasts. Eventually, a new breed of canal resident emerged, celebrating an "anything goes" and "peace and love" state of mind.

The city of Los Angeles proposed various schemes for redeveloping the canals. But the local residents angrily fought any such plans. They feared that the city would destroy the egalitarian character of the community by replacing it with an exclusive, high-rise extension of the Marina. When the canal residents organized and publicly demonstrated against redevelopment, the city abandoned its projects and the canals won another reprieve.

Various signs of renewal emerged in the 1970's. Old-timers began to clean up the canals and footpaths. Newcomers repaired ramshackle bungalows, built innovatively designed homes, and handsomely landscaped their properties. However, as wealthy settlers continue to buy up real estate, many long-time Venetians fear that gentrification will squeeze out poorer residents and disrupt the diverse nature of the canal neighborhood.

As you stroll along the canals, hundreds of ducks, geese, and swans will greet you, loudly badgering for handouts of stale bread. Watch your step, as many of the old concrete sidewalk slabs have crumbled or fallen into the water. Below are highlighted only a few of the scores of noteworthy residences. Take time to appreciate the picturesque detail and character of this unique village.

9. John's Market Mural

Dell Avenue and South Venice Boulevard
A landmark in the canal community, this neighborhood grocery chronicles Venice's hippie era (1965–1975) with a mural by the Women's Collective along Dell Avenue. Study the mural scene: the story of the late '60's canal folk unfolds.

10. House (1982)

401 Dell Avenue
This hand crafted English cottage, with its half-timbers and stained glass windows, reflects the residential renaissance of the canals.

Venice's canal neighborhood, with its arching bridges and placid waterways, provides a serene retreat from the beachfront crowds.

11. House (1982)

237 Carroll Canal
Another sign of renewal and whimsy, this neo-Victorian abode faces the serenity of Carroll Canal.

12. Grand Canal

between North Venice Boulevard and Marina del Rey
The major water artery connecting the Pacific with the interior canals. Dredged in 1904, the channel is a half-mile long, four feet deep, and thirty feet wide.

13. Venice Canals Children's Park

Linnie Canal and Dell Avenue

In 1973 a number of canal residents, many of them hippies, commandeered an empty plot of city-owned land and built a playground for their children. After many confrontations and court battles, the city of Los Angeles finally designated it legally as a children's playground. Amusingly, a small canal flows through the park into Linnie Canal.

14. House (1982)

2415 Eastern Canal

A first-rate Post-modern residence, highlighted by exposed steel support beams, industrial steel grating as interior walkways, translucent glass-brick walls, and stark white sides.

15. House (1980)

240 Howland Canal

Its rounded roof resembling the hull of an overturned ship, this Post-modern design might also be labeled as nautical neo-Deco. Note the variety of window styles and balconies as it overshadows the waterway.

16. Bungalow Court (ca. 1915)

236 Howland Canal

Original housecourt of vacation rentals, now apartments.

MARINA DEL REY

The modern high-rises of Marina del Rey loom over the landscape southeast of Washington Street. Before this encroachment of urban development in the late 1960's, the Ballona Creek Wetlands formed a marshy inlet where the Ballona Creek emptied into the Pacific. At the estuary large sand dunes created a peninsula which buffered the wetlands from the sea.

Once the estuary sheltered bountiful game, fish, and fowl. For centuries local Indians frequented the area to hunt game, collect shells, and gather medicinal herbs. Several Gabrieleno Indian villages were situated along the Venice and Playa del Rey bluffs overlooking the tidal basin.

As Spanish, Mexican, and American settlers migrated to Los Angeles, small hunting expeditions visited the marshes. Several hunting lodges were built in the late 1800's, but the wetlands remained undeveloped.

In the mid-1920's, oil was discovered in the area. Almost overnight hundreds of makeshift oil wells appeared throughout the peninsula. A forest of derricks and pumps encroached upon houses and yards. Most of the marshes, however, proved too swampy for such exploitation.

In the 1950's developers presented several proposals for the wetlands. Los Angeles County finally authorized a large-scale plan for developing an extensive small-craft harbor and adjoining commercial and residential areas. Built between 1958 and 1966, and officially dedicated on April 10, 1965, Marina del Rey is a formidable, but uninspired, statement of modern development. In its concrete basin over ten thousand pleasure craft find refuge. Extensive apartment and hotel complexes, restaurants, bars, discos, and shopping centers attract a young, single, professional crowd. While this walk only skirts the Marina, you may want to return to explore its harbor.

17. Baja Cantina and Siamese Gardens

311 Washington Street

These two eateries reflect the type of dining experience which is popular in the Marina. Both offer outdoor patios, creative ethnic menus, attractive crowds, and casual dining.

18. Washington Street Commercial District

between Grand Canal and Ocean Front Walk

Along these several blocks thrive businesses which cater to beach people from both the posh Marina and funky Venice. Bikini boutiques, surf shops, outdoor cafes, art galleries, and bike and roller-skate rental shops abound.

19. House

11 Anchorage Street

Rudolf Valentino, silent movie idol, lived in this beach house in the 1920's.

20. Venice Fishing Pier

at the end of Washington Street

Built in 1965, this public pier hosts hundreds of city folk as they fish daily for rock cod, bonita, halibut, and mackerel. From its curvilinear end, you can survey the coastline from Palos Verdes to Malibu.

OCEAN FRONT WALK
between Washington Street and Windward Avenue

Stretching between the Venice and Santa Monica piers, this popular promenade attracts every type of urbanite. Beachcombers, joggers, poets, tourists, urban castaways, families on roller skates, suave singles, and skateboarders romp and roll along the boardwalk.

As you meander along the Walk, note the variety of beach houses and apartments. Sit awhile on a bench and watch the circus. Or even rent a pair of skates and glide the boardwalk. Eventually you will come to the paddleball courts, an outdoor weightlifting club, and a gymnastic sand area, as well as art galleries, folk craft displays, and fast food stands.

21. West Beach Cafe

60 North Venice Boulevard

One of L.A.'s outstanding nouvelle California cafes. The white, skylit, airy interior provides an ambiance of casual yet elegant dining, and works by local artists grace the high-tech interior.

22. L.A. Louver Gallery

55 North Venice Boulevard

Behind the tiled entryway, works by both well-known and emerging artists await viewing.

For Further Reading on Venice:

Tom Moran and Tom Sewell, *Fantasy by the Sea,* 1980
Ann Nietzke, *Windowlight: A Woman's Journal from the Edge of America,* 1982
Jeffrey Stanton, *Venice of America 1905–1930,* 1980
Sweet William, *Venice of America: The American Dream Come True,* 1976

MANHATTAN BEACH WALKS

etween the bluffs of Playa del Rey and the hills of Palos Verdes Peninsula is an urban region known as the South Bay. This coastal area includes the cities of El Segundo, Manhattan Beach, Hermosa Beach, Redondo Beach, and Torrance. Ocean breezes keep these cities free of hot temperatures and smog. Busy LAX, major oil refineries, power generating plants, and aerospace corporations employ thousands of local technicians and professionals. Attracted by the pleasant beaches, quiet residential neighborhoods, and robust industries, over a quarter of a million people live in the South Bay. Each of its cities offers inviting settings for urban walking.

But of all the South Bay cities, one community stands apart as an alluring and captivating place for citywalking. With lively contrasts of character found in its distinct villages, Manhattan Beach offers a variety of colorful lifestyles as well as neighborhoods for exploration.

In the beach side of town, you encounter the quintessential beach culture with its hang-loose, easygoing lifestyle of surfing, volleyball, jogging, and beach bumming. In the north end, evening throngs of young singles party at the dance bars and cafes. Inland, young families adopt a lifestyle which epitomizes the California Dream of casual, yet elegant, suburban living. And downtown surprises visitors with a genuine feeling of small town friendliness as locals chat with one another and strangers greet you with smiles and hellos.

Manhattan Beach — today crowded, friendly, and compact — is a new town. Only a hundred years ago, the coastal area was barren and deserted. Shifting sand dunes rose up to two hundred feet above the windswept shoreline. For several miles the snaking sand ridge continued south, gradually leveling near Hermosa Beach. Just inland past the steep dunes, small hollows of brackish water were found. About one-half mile beyond the beach, gentle grassy hills undulated inland.

In 1888 the Santa Fe Railroad, recognizing the economic potential of the South Bay, built a line from Los Angeles to Redondo Beach. Later a small substation was constructed near present Manhattan Beach Boulevard and called "Shore Acres." By 1900 the sandy dunes of Manhattan Beach began to attract real estate speculators and promoters.

Stuart Merrill, a native New Yorker, platted the southern section of the townsite below Manhattan Beach Boulevard in 1902. To ease walking along the sandy slopes, Merrill placed wooden planks along Manhattan Avenue and the Strand in 1905. Because of his origin and the town's proximity to the sea, he named his portion "Manhattan."

The central portion between Marine Avenue and Manhattan Beach Boulevard was developed by Frank Dougherty and five associates. They called their corporation the "Highland Beach Company," and brought five hundred Angelenos on a chartered train to promote their grand opening in 1902.

The area north of Marine Avenue was developed by George Peck. Platting the sloping dunes between the Strand and the ridge crest, Peck named his tract "Shore Acres" after the Santa Fe substation.

As land sales increased and the three developments began to merge, the promoters in 1903 decided to choose a common name for the new town. Merrill pressed for the name "Manhattan" and Peck for "Shore Acres." They flipped a half dollar and Merrill won. In 1927, the town's postmaster petitioned postal authorities to have "Beach" added to

distinguish the South Bay city from fourteen other towns called "Manhattan."

In 1904 a local interurban electric transit line was added between Marina del Rey and Redondo Beach, spurring further growth throughout the South Bay. Running along the coast, the transit line included four local stops, each with a wooden pier and two with recreational facilities. More boardwalks and planks were laid to aid travel within Manhattan.

The town's first houses were nothing more than simple wooden cottages, some better described as shacks. Yet new residences continued to be built, and in 1909 two civic organizations were formed. One, the Manhattan Beach Improvement Association, consisted of local merchants and businesspeople. The other, an assembly of local women called the Neptunian Club, was dedicated to civic improvement through education, recreation, beautification, and social gatherings. Both organizations pressed for cityhood. In 1912, the five hundred residents of Manhattan voted to incorporate as a city.

Since 1975 Manhattan Beach has experienced a period of remarkable revitalization. Younger families, single professionals, and wealthier suburbanites have moved into older tract houses, particularly near the beach. Rents and housing costs have increased dramatically, forcing less wealthy residents to move. Old houses are being remodeled into decorator showcases. New residences are being built, reflecting styles from whimsical neo-Victorian townhouses to stark Post-modern monuments.

As an urban community, Manhattan Beach today is best described as a small town in the midst of a metropolis. The city's residents evince a solid commitment to encouraging a neighborly, active, and conscientious town. Each October residents participate in the Hometown Fair, which includes baseball games, a chili cook-off, and a ten kilometer run. During the summer, the city hosts the Surf Festival, beach volleyball tournaments, and the Grand Prix bike race. Sunday afternoon concerts in Polliwog Park present free summer music to the townsfolk, who picnic and play on the lawns.

These two walks explore the various villages within Manhattan Beach. The first tour proceeds from the downtown area to a portion of the Hill Section, where medium-sized homes overlook the South Bay and Palos Verdes. Then the tour zigzags through the Sand Section, examining the well landscaped and beautifully designed residential architecture. Returning to downtown and the pier, the walk then glides along the Strand and the beach. Leading up the ridge, the tour then descends into Live Oak Park, follows the railroad tracks, and explores the quiet, shady Tree Section and its large homes. Returning to downtown, you can leisurely enjoy an early dinner or relax on the pier.

The second walk begins in the business area of the northern Sand Section, with its funky cafes, posh restaurants, singles bars, and surf shops. Climbing the sand ridge, the walk then leads down the steep slope of Sand Dunes Park and into the northern Tree Section and the Gaslight Section, where small, mundane tract houses have been imaginatively remodeled and the narrow streets lined with ornate gaslights. The tour passes through Live Oak Park, up the ridge, and down to the Strand. From there the route follows the beach to El Porto, the northernmost village of Manhattan Beach. Finally, after a hilly walk, you can relax at a cafe or restaurant in the business section.

SOUTH MANHATTAN BEACH WALK

1. Civic Center
2. Criterion Restaurant
3. Uncle Bill's Pancake House
4. Beach Books
5. Talia's
6. Cookie Post
7. The Kettle Restaurant
8. The Koffee Kart
9. Hennessey's Tavern
10. Cafe Pierre
11. Metlox Site
12. Manhattan Beach Substation Sign
13. Gamesfield Fitness Course
14. Residential Landscaping
15. Townhouses
16. Neo-Georgian House
17. Townhouses
18. Townhouses
19. Atchison House
20. Anderson House
21. Shields House
22. Moderne House
23. Runyon House
24. The Strand
25. Craftsman Style Houses
26. Townhouses
27. Early House
28. Courtney's Restaurant
29. Perri's Wine and Tobacco Shop
30. Becker's Bakery
31. Ercole's
32. Hibachi
33. Shellback Tavern
34. Manhattan Beach Municipal Pier
35. Townhouses
36. Eighteenth Street
37. Live Oak Park
38. Joslyn Community Center
39. Williams House
40. American Martyrs Catholic Church
41. Manhattan Beach Historical Society

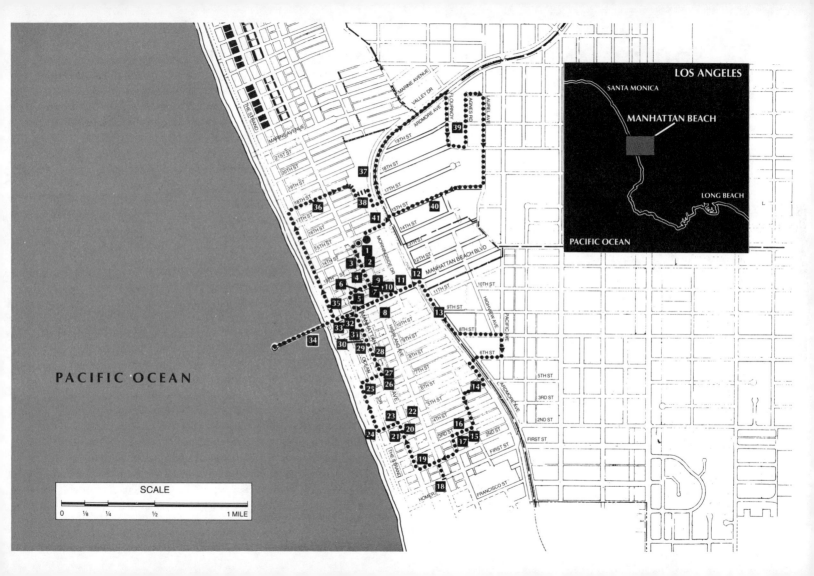

PACIFIC OCEAN

SCALE

0   ⅛   ¼   ½   1 MILE

LOS ANGELES

SANTA MONICA

MANHATTAN BEACH

LONG BEACH

PACIFIC OCEAN

SOUTH MANHATTAN BEACH WALK

DIRECTIONS: *From I-405 (San Diego Freeway), exit west on Rosecrans Avenue. Follow to Highland Avenue and turn left (south). Follow to Manhattan Beach Boulevard and turn left to Valley Drive/Ardmore Avenue.*

PARKING: *Weekend parking is scarce. Plan to beat the weekend beach crowds and park before 9 a.m. by the railroad tracks near Manhattan Beach Boulevard.*

PUBLIC TRANSPORTATION: *RTD lines 861, 871.*

DISTANCE: *A hilly, challenging three miles.*

DURATION: *Allow a leisurely four hours, including breakfast.*

SUGGESTED ITINERARY: *Start at Highland Avenue and Fifteenth Street, and have breakfast at Uncle Bill's, the Criterion, the Kettle, or the Koffee Kart, all of which are lively, popular cafes among local townsfolk.*

CLOTHES: *Shorts, sandals, and tank tops.*

DOWNTOWN MANHATTAN BEACH

In 1902 Stuart Merrill laid large wooden planks along steep sand dunes to create Manhattan Beach Boulevard, then called Center Street. Over the decades, as the South Bay town grew, the street was paved and small stores crowded between the Santa Fe Railroad substation and the Pacific Electric trolley station on the Strand. Commercial areas spread along Highland and Manhattan avenues as well, forming a condensed, compact center for the small town.

Today, the railroad and trolley cars have disappeared, but downtown Manhattan Beach continues to convey the sense of a small town's commercial core. Shopkeepers often live nearby and walk to work. Shoppers and proprietors often greet one another by first name and catch up on the local news. Reflecting the casual beach culture, most downtown visitors walk from store to store in shorts, thongs, and polo or tropical print shirts. Carrying boogie boards, skateboards, and towels, teenagers hurry from the bus stops to the beach, stopping by Hibachi for soft drinks on the way. Everyone seems to be tanned and energetic. Downtown Manhattan Beach is the commercial center of a quaint, casual, friendly community.

1. **Civic Center** (1975)
   1300 block of Highland Avenue
   Both the modern city hall and the spacious public library, designed by the architectural firm of H. Wendell Mounce and Associates, provide extensive public services in comfortable surroundings. Inside the city hall lobby stands a

two-story-high mural by Mexican artist Miguel Angel Velaquez. Donated to the city in 1975 by the people of Culiacán, Mexico, the imposing mural projects a sculptural effect with its textured epoxies and nitro-cellulose lacquers. The entry to the public library contains an unassuming glazed-tile mural by L. A. Whitten depicting the clouds, hills, sand, and sea.

2. Criterion Restaurant

1300 Highland Avenue

This twenty-four-hour restaurant contains a mishmash of styles, from a mission-style belltower to brass nautical table lanterns and an outdoor patio. The menu ranges from huevos rancheros, omelettes, and fresh baked pies to fresh seafood. A mural on the rear wall, painted by Stephanie Taylor and Judy Anderson in 1980, presents a startling portrait of downtown Manhattan Beach underwater.

3. Uncle Bill's Pancake House

1305 Highland Avenue

Lines of weekend brunchers patiently sit, read, and people watch as they wait for seating in this cozy, friendly cottage cafe. Originally a patio for the adjacent house, Uncle Bill's has been a popular breakfast and lunch spot since the 1950's. The newest owner, Paul Van Amburgh, has retained its funky decor of framed menus, faded cartoons of past regulars, and cushioned stools around a low counter. Cheerful, folksy waitresses serve breakfasts of huge omelettes accompanied by a choice of toast, pancakes, or homemade muffins, in flavors from blueberry, banana, pineapple, or cinnamon to the more inventive peanut butter or brandy raisin. A reservations sign-up sheet is just inside the front door.

4. Beach Books

1205 Highland Avenue

Proprietor Gwen Henry, a city resident for over twenty years, believes that a local bookstore should be more than just a shop for best sellers and paperbacks. Vivacious and helpful, Gwen allows her store to be a clearing house for local information and a rendezvous for community groups. Local customers often meet and chat about town issues and events in her shop. And Gwen's shelves contain a little bit of everything, from hard-to-find books to current best sellers.

5. Talia's

1148 Manhattan Avenue

Owner Ronald Guidone's cozy restaurant serves excellent regional Italian dishes. Moderately priced entrees, always fresh and imaginative, are accompanied by an extensive list of carefully selected California and imported wines. Sunday brunch is served from 8 a.m. to 2:30 p.m.

6. Cookie Post

1142 Manhattan Avenue

When the city opened a new post office, locals fought to save the old structure, a downtown landmark since 1940. In 1977 the old brick building was converted into the Cookie Post, an innovative bakery which today maintains the 315 original oak paneled, antique brass post office boxes in the lobby. Antique tables, ceiling fans, and oak display cases create a nostalgic setting for sweet-toothed customers. Owners Dick Martinez and Frank Ross daily bake a variety of mouth-watering cookies, including chocolate chip, oatmeal raisin, peanut butter, and snickerdoodles, all of which are sold by the pound. The Cookie Post also serves Dreyer's ice cream and stuffed croissants.

7. The Kettle Restaurant

1138 Highland Avenue

Another popular twenty-four-hour restaurant, the Kettle offers a wide variety of menu items from fresh fruit salads and omelettes to appetizers and thick sandwiches. A busy, friendly cafe, the Kettle is frequented by a diverse mix of locals, from surfers to businesspeople.

8. The Koffee Kart

1104 Highland Avenue

In 1968 Lois Wood and Edith Bierer, two long-time waitresses at Uncle Bill's, decided to open their own breakfast nook and began this unpretentious cafe. Through the years, Lois and Edith have succeeded in establishing a satisfying, popular restaurant, serving nearly fifty varieties of omelettes and home baked muffins and biscuits. The cinnamon apple pancakes and the stroganoff omelette with sour cream are local favorites. But just the pleasure of sitting in this neighborhood cafe is worthwhile, enjoying the friendly service and clientele, where everyone seems to know everyone else.

9. Hennessey's Tavern

313 Manhattan Beach Boulevard

Hennessey's which also owns Hermosa's Lighthouse Jazz Club and three other South Bay pubs, opened this tavern in 1982. The menu offers a variety of half-pound hamburgers, sandwiches, and salads. To quench an Irishman's thirst, the pub serves Guinness draft, as well as Beck's, Harp Irish lager, and its famous Irish coffee.

10. Cafe Pierre

317 Manhattan Beach Boulevard

This quaint country French cafe, owned by Guy Gabriele, offers a wide-ranging moderately priced bill of fare, from fish, veal, and chicken to its own baked pastries. Entrees are accompanied by a discerning list of nearly a hundred wines. Recently, Cafe Pierre opened a wine bar offering glasses of finer wines as well as appetizers, desserts, and cappuccino. Once a month an evening is devoted to a programmed dinner with guest winemakers. Sunday brunch is served from 10:30 a.m. to 2:30 p.m.

11. Metlox Site

1100 block of Morningside Drive

For decades Metlox, creators of Poppytrail dinnerware, pottery, and artware, was the major employer in Manhattan Beach. Since 1947 Metlox occupied this site, its open air market and retail yard a local landmark. But in 1983 the company sold its frontage on Manhattan Beach Boulevard and planned to rebuild its operation in Torrance. A hotel and restaurants are planned for this site.

ARDMORE-VALLEY CORRIDOR

In 1888, the Santa Fe Railroad extended its line from Los Angeles to Redondo Beach through this valley. A substation was built at Center Street, providing companies such as Metlox with ready rail transport to inland markets. Today, however, the trains no longer run, and the Santa Fe right-of-way is used for parking lots, green space, and jogging trails. Various proposals await decisions, from the controversial South Bay Trolley to scenic parkland. Currently, the tracks lie rusting, and landscaping has been initiated by local residents, who have planted lawns, oleander bushes, eucalyptus trees, and iceplant.

12. **Manhattan Beach Substation Sign**
    Valley Drive at Manhattan Beach Boulevard
    This fading wooden sign marks the 1888 site of the Santa Fe substation, a significant landmark in the city's history.

13. **Gamesfield Fitness Course**
    Valley Drive at Eleventh Street
    Reflecting the physical fitness craze in Southern California, the city built this total body conditioning circuit, which includes self-guided programs for running, stretching, body building, and weight loss.

SAND SECTION

Sloping uphill from the wide beach to the railroad tracks is an area called the Sand Section. As settlers arrived and began to build their homes here, the steep slopes and unstable sand demanded special problem-solving in both residential and landscape architecture.

In the 1920's, after the city hired contractors to level the steep ridges and fill in the shifting hollows, streets were laid. Winds often created deep sand drifts which buried many streets nearly to the top of lampposts. Sands shifted, undermining boardwalks and houses. Deep hollows interrupted travel and building.

The northern dune section proved more stable than the southern ridge. In the 1920's the city hired contractors to move large portions of the southern dunes between Manhattan Beach Boulevard and First Street. Large tractors worked for months pushing the unstable sand ridge into hollows. But the steep grades remained on the hillsides near the beach. City planners then designed most streets leading down the hill to the ocean as pedestrian pathways; streets paralleling the beach were planned for auto traffic.

As foundations for houses were dug, many builders relied upon pilings and later used cement blocks to secure the structures. Sand was transported away from yards; soil and humus were shipped in. To prevent the sandy slopes from eroding, ground cover was planted. In some situations, builders laid bricks or constructed concrete and wooden decks to secure the sand. By the end of the decade, the dunes were rounded and excess sand had been sold to construction companies for projects as diverse as cement for the Coliseum to beach sand for Waikiki.

The lots in the Sand Section are small and densely packed with houses. Most houses extend nearly to the property line, maximizing lot space. Such density seems to evoke a strong need to identify territory; most houses mark their property with fences, walls, and other boundaries.

Many houses are designed to take full advantage of the fine ocean breezes and views. Averaging two or three stories, they have balconies, verandas, decks, rooftop gardens, porches, patios, or wide picture windows. And windmills, flags, and pennants seem to celebrate the refreshing, cleansing sea breezes.

During the past decade, property values have soared as wealthier newcomers have settled in the Sand Section. Whole blocks of weathered houses have been renovated, while some structures have been demolished and replaced with architectural showcases. No longer can students and young singles easily afford the luxury of seaside living in Manhattan Beach.

Even with these changes, the Sand Section continues to be a friendly, conscientious neighborhood. Residents often take early evening strolls, greeting one another by first name. Gardens and houses are meticulously tended. There is a sense of urban camaraderie and homespun pride among the Sand People which enriches the small town character of Manhattan Beach.

14. Residential Landscaping
Fifth Street between Valley Drive and Ingleside Drive
The town's footpaths are often wide promenades bordered by tidy fenced yards. An amazing variety of vegetation creates an arboretum-like setting on many blocks. With its low picket fences and front patios, Fifth Street illustrates this landscaping diversity with the following flora: Mexican fan palms (at number 541), olives (536), Brazilian pepper trees (529), Indian laurel fig trees (524), Hollywood junipers (521), pink melanleucas (520), magnolia, jacaranda, and orange pittosporum (516), evergreen pear and melanleucas (517), Italian stone pine (513), hibiscus (505), red gum eucalyptus (437), and California sycamore and bougainvillaea at 501 Fourth Street.

15. Townhouses (1983)
1710 Morningside Drive
Modern three-story French provincial townhouses with mansard roof, gables, French doors, and decorative iron grille balconies.

16. House (ca. 1950)
326 Second Street
Neo-Georgian colonial tract house with a columned front, shuttered windows, and classical detailing around the door and entablatures.

17. Townhouses (1983)
320 Second Street
Three-story modern townhouses, San Francisco Edwardian in character with simple bay windows.

18. Townhouses (1980)
95–97 Highland Avenue
Twin three-story Mediterranean villas, charmingly decorated with exposed support beams, intricate grillwork, adobe tiling, private balconies, and thick stucco walls.

19. Atchison House (1983)
201 Third Street
An outstanding example of new residential architecture in the South Bay, this house, designed by Mark Appel, might best be called ''Beach high-tech.'' The bold flat surfaces and metal chutes of industrial high-tech design are softened with glass blocks, stained glass windows, natural grained wood detailing, and jade green tinted windows.

20. Anderson House (1982)
400 Manhattan Avenue

Reminiscent of San Francisco's Victorian masterpieces, these townhouses, designed by the owner and contractor York Bourgeois, create a whimsical image. Mrs.Anderson, who longed to own a Victorian house in the South Bay, studied Victorian architecture and worked out these designs, detailed with hand crafted corbels, moldings, latticed corner porches, etched glass, and bay windows.

21. Shields House (ca. 1925)
132 Fourth Street

This house has been imaginatively remodeled into a rustic neo-Victorian lodge, playfully detailed with a shingled conical tower, stained glass windows, and a weather vane.

22. House (ca. 1935)
207 Fifth Street

This two-story, terraced house presents a bold blend of Zigzag Moderne and Pueblo Revival with its embossed horizontal bands.

23. Runyon House (1980)
121 Fifth Street

Owner Robert Runyon, designer of the 1984 Los Angeles Olympics logo, describes his house as ''tongue-in-cheek Western Victorian.'' He extrapolated the overall design from an extensive Victorian architecture library. Hand crafted inside and out, its brilliantly colored shingles, wind-snapped

Reminiscent of San Francisco's Victorian masterpieces, the Anderson House reveals the recent trend of new playful residential architecture in Manhattan Beach.

flags, and decorative fittings attract many appreciative and amused admirers. This house was also the first neo-Victorian residence in town, starting the trend in such architecture.

24. The Strand
between Fifth and Eighth Streets

This wide oceanfront walkway follows what once was a sandy Indian footpath. Now the well lighted concrete promenade, with its sweeping views of Santa Monica Bay, is enjoyed by walkers, joggers, and skaters. In 1902 local real estate promoters built long walkways of wooden planks along the beachfront. An interurban electric trolley, built in 1904,

followed the wooden pathway, which was finally replaced by the concrete walk in 1918. In the mid-1970's, the parallel bikeway was built, guiding cyclists between Redondo Beach and Santa Monica.

25. Houses (ca. 1910–1915)

712–800 The Strand

These Craftsman Style beach cottages, some of which were built from scrap lumber, were among the first residences in Manhattan Beach. Resting on redwood pilings, the shingled wooden structures command panoramic views of the bay.

26. Townhouses (1981)

708 Manhattan Avenue

Neo-Victorian townhouses designed by York Bourgeois, these residences are evidence of the stylistic playfulness of architectural design in L.A. Bourgeois also designed 620 Manhattan Avenue, another neo-Victorian house with country French detailing.

27. House (1902)

712 Manhattan Avenue

The oldest house in Manhattan Beach, this beach shack was built amidst barren sand dunes.

28. Courtney's Restaurant

900 Manhattan Avenue

A warm, rustic, yet elegant restaurant serving ''South Bay continental'' cuisine, Courtney's offers a dining experience which exemplifies the best of South Bay living. Chalet-esque

Built in 1980, the Runyon House at 121 Fifth Street is a whimsically styled neo-Victorian house with Eastlake detailing.

in character, with its flower boxes, lace curtains, and weathered wood, the restaurant contains Gothic stained glass windows from a hundred-year-old Episcopal church in Wisconsin. The wood sidings are from reclaimed Oregon barn wood. With live music in its cozy lounge, Courtney's upstairs dining room specializes in fresh seafood, duck, chicken, and curried dishes, as well as home baked pastries.

29. Perri's Wine and Tobacco Shop
1009 Manhattan Avenue

If you've never stopped and browsed in a tobacco shop before, you've missed a delightful experience. Perri's offers the largest selection of pipes, tobaccos, and cigars in the South Bay. Paul and Margaret Perri, the chatty owners, display a large selection of pipes, ranging from a corncob pipe costing $1.50 to hand carved burlwood briars for over $500. But the real treat in exploring the shop are the forty or so custom tobacco blends prepared by Paul and displayed in glass jars. A secret blend unique to the South Bay is the Beachcomber, a sweet fruity cavendish (although Margaret wouldn't say, a scent of coconut seems evident).

30. Becker's Bakery
1025 Manhattan Avenue

In 1942, when ''Pappy'' Becker opened this small bakery, Manhattan Beach acquired a fastidious baker committed to Old World breadmaking. Trained by German bakers, Pappy expanded his selections and made an acclaimed buttercrust and seven-grain squaw bread, as well as delicately prepared black forest, German chocolate, and carrot cakes. Now,

nearly half a century and two generations later, the Becker family continues to bake breads, pies, cakes, and cookies with an old fashioned concern for quality and care. Stop inside and say hello to Allie Nelson, who for twenty years has served Manhattanites with a courteous smile and generous service.

31. Ercoles
1101 Manhattan Avenue

The oldest bar in Manhattan Beach, Ercoles opened as a small cafe during Prohibition. Since then the bar has assumed the character of a Greenwich Village pub, with its 1950's photos of jazz sessions and the smoke-stained walls covered with wetted graffiti.

32. Hibachi
120 Manhattan Beach Boulevard

From the street, the window counter appears to be just another fast food stand. But walk down the narrow passageway and you'll discover a friendly, inexpensive, beach cafe specializing in Japanese-American food. The garden patio is decorated with Japanese lanterns, vine-covered trellises, brightly painted potted plants, and picnic tables. Owner Frank Nam serves an eclectic mix of drinks, from domestic and Japanese beers (Kirin, Asahi, and Sapporo) to sweet tropical concoctions (mai tais, Kona grogs, and sake margaritas). Lunches include hefty dishes of char-broiled burgers, teriyaki steaks, seafood salads, and the popular stir-fry chicken (with mushrooms, snow peas, water chestnuts, sprouts, celery, and onions). For dinner sample the suiami, teriyaki halibut, sukiyaki, swordfish kabobs, or yaki niku.

33. Shellback Tavern

116 Manhattan Beach Boulevard

A British-style pub, the Shellback offers food as well as pints of Guinness and games of darts. Windows provide generous views of the beach and pier. The bloody marys, made with a secret recipe, and the chili, winner of both the 1979 and 1981 Hometown Fair chili cook-off, are the best bets.

34. Manhattan Beach Municipal Pier (1921)

foot of Manhattan Beach Boulevard

This concrete pier provides townspeople with sweeping views, fishing facilities, and public restrooms. The round structure at the end houses an oceanographic study program for schoolchildren. Surveying the northern bay, you can spot tankers delivering oil to power generating plants, air traffic gliding over LAX, sailboats leaving Marina del Rey, white towers marking downtown Santa Monica, and the rugged Santa Monica Mountains rising above the Malibu coast. To the south you can view the Hermosa Beach Pier, Redondo Beach's King Harbor, and the terraced hills of Palos Verdes Peninsula. On clear days Santa Catalina Island, thirty-one miles offshore, etches the horizon, luring yachts to its romantic coves and inlets. Closer to the pier, young surfers paddle out and wait for the "perfect" wave. Watching the surfers can be exhilarating as they skillfully and playfully maneuver among the waves. At the end of the pier, steadfast anglers wait for the "big one," their buckets displaying catches of bonita, mackerel, and occasionally eel or octopus.

35. Townhouses (1981)

1144 The Strand

These three-story Queen Anne style neo-Victorian townhouses, with their ornate scrollwork and corner tower, add to the town's growing colony of San Francisco-inspired architecture.

36. Eighteenth Street

between The Strand and Highland Avenue

Reminiscent of San Francisco's Lombard Street, this walkway zigzags as it climbs the steep hillside. An interesting mix of residential architecture fronts the pathway, from humble beach cottages to contemporary "mineshaft" houses of weathered wood and rustic decor, the landscaping terraced with railroad ties.

37. Live Oak Park

bounded by Valley Drive, Seventeenth and Twenty-third Streets

Climbing up the sand ridge, Eighteenth Street leads to a stairpath which descends into Live Oak Park, an urban green filled with recreational facilities from tennis courts to baseball diamonds. Walk to the right (south) above the basketball courts to the Seventeenth Street stairpath and down through the park to Valley Drive.

38. Joslyn Community Center (1965)

1601 Valley Drive

Dedicated to the senior citizens of Manhattan Beach in 1965, this well managed and designed community center provides a wide range of recreational, educational, and cultural activities.

The flat rocks used in the entrance hall are Palos Verdes flagstone, a popular material for building facades.

TREE SECTION

Since the 1890's, small farms and tree-lined fields created a rural district in the gentle hills east of the railroad tracks. As Manhattan Beach grew in the 1930's, developers purchased land in this area and built squat tract houses. Fortunately, most of the large eucalyptus trees, originally planted as windbreaks, were spared and used as shade trees for the new homes. This neighborhood has since become known as the Tree Section.

Many new residents have settled in the Tree Section since 1975. Exhibiting the spirit of urban pioneers, these young families have remodeled and refurbished many of the once tacky tract houses into handsomely designed residences evocative of Brentwood and Newport Beach. Some homes reflect a more traditional Mediterranean or Norman styling, while others celebrate the idiosyncratic designs of imaginative owners.

The Tree Section has become a stylish, quiet, family neighborhood. Two elementary schools and the landmark American Martyrs Catholic Church are surrounded by tree-shaded lanes and large homes. As you walk in this village, observe the variety of well-kept residential and landscape architecture, as well as the friendliness and casualness of the residents.

39. Williams House
1825 Agnes Road
Originally a mundane stucco tract house, this residence has been remodeled into a fanciful "Calico Gold Rush" lodge. The rustic, weathered front suggests a mining camp manor. Inside, owner Joe Williams has decorated the house with many recycled ornaments, including a stained glass window from Torrance High School, balconies from the Barlow Sanitarium in Elysian Park, brass handrails from the old Mutual Pacific Building in downtown Los Angeles, and a bedroom door from the Coca-Cola Bottling Company conference room.

40. American Martyrs Catholic Church (1956)
Fifteenth and Church Streets
Atop the crest of a hill, this imposing church may be seen from throughout the city. Inside the modern brick structure are beautiful stained glass windows and numerous statues. Along Fifteenth Street stand sculptures of heroic Catholic mission and church workers who were martyred in North America.

41. Manhattan Beach Historical Society
425 Fifth Street
An independent nonprofit organization, this community group is dedicated "to investigate, collect, catalogue, and maintain records and memorabilia and to disseminate this information to interested persons and groups." Among the old photos, records, and other artifacts are a series of outstanding booklets on facets of Manhattan Beach's history. Open to the public on Tuesdays and Thursdays, 1–5 p.m.

1. The Beach Hut
2. Jo Anne's Chili Bordello
3. Orville and Wilbur's
4. Bruce Grant Surfboards
5. Frank's Bar and Grill
6. Pancho's Restaurant
7. Brennan's
8. Sloopy's Beach Cafe
9. Ron's Nonnos Cafe
10. House
11. Sand Dunes Park
12. Grandview Palms
13. Live Oak Park
14. Eighteenth Street
15. Villa Oceana
16. House
17. Townhouses
18. House and Succulent Garden
19. Black-Roloff House
20. County Department of Beaches and Harbor
21. Duncan House
22. House
23. House
24. Howe House

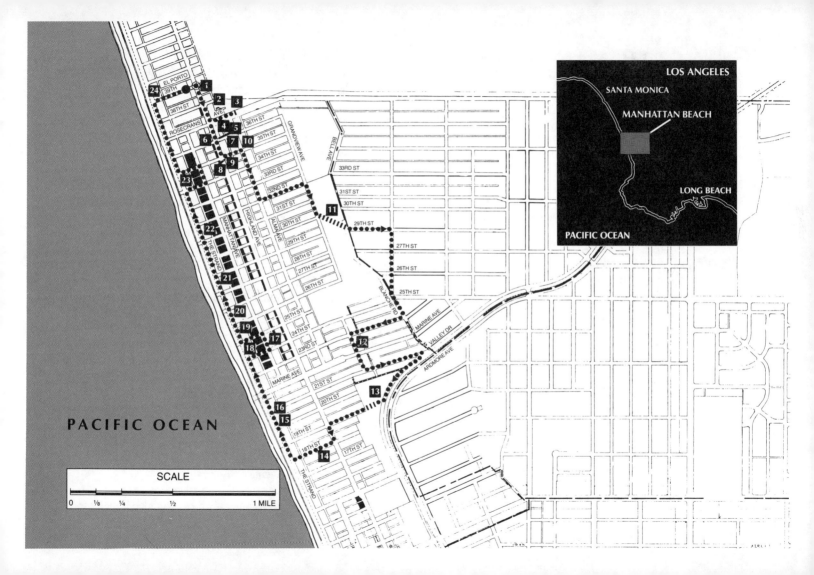

PACIFIC OCEAN

SCALE

0   ⅛   ¼   ½   1 MILE

EL PORTO
39TH
38TH ST
ROSECRANS AVE
36TH ST
35TH ST
34TH ST
33RD ST
32ND ST
31ST ST
30TH ST
29TH ST
28TH ST
27TH ST
26TH ST
25TH ST
24TH ST
23RD ST
21ST ST
20TH ST
19TH ST
18TH ST
17TH ST

GRANDVIEW AVE
BELL AVE
HIGHLAND AVE
ALMA AVE
MANHATTAN AVE
THE STRAND
MARINE AVE

33RD ST
31ST ST
30TH ST
29TH ST
27TH ST
26TH ST
25TH ST

BLANCHARD

MARINE AVE
VALLEY DR
ARDMORE AVE
THE STRAND

LOS ANGELES
SANTA MONICA
MANHATTAN BEACH
LONG BEACH
PACIFIC OCEAN

NORTH MANHATTAN BEACH WALK

DIRECTIONS: *From I-405 (San Diego Freeway), exit west on Rosecrans Avenue. Follow to Highland Avenue and park near this intersection.*

PARKING: *On weekends, public parking is scarce by noon; it's best to arrive by 10 a.m. Some of the side streets east of Highland Avenue often have available, free parking.*

PUBLIC TRANSPORTATION: *RTD lines 42, 126, 438.*

DISTANCE: *About two miles.*

DURATION: *A casual four hours, including breakfast and perhaps lunch.*

SUGGESTED ITINERARY: *Start on Highland Avenue at Thirty-ninth Street; stop for a Hawaiian breakfast fit for surfers at the Beach Hut, or a more conventional breakfast at Ron's Nonnos Cafe; both of these cafes cater to local folk. After the walk, you might want to spend the rest of the afternoon at the beach and later enjoy an early dinner at Pancho's or another local restaurant.*

NORTH END BUSINESS SECTION
Highland Avenue between 41st Street and 34th Street

In 1902, as real estate speculation in Southern California spread to the South Bay, George Peck purchased this area and platted the sand dunes into small lots. When the interurban electric trolley line was extended along the Strand from Playa del Rey to Redondo Beach in 1904, land values soared. Peck zoned this stretch of Highland Avenue to be the primary commercial district for northern Manhattan Beach.

The small businesses cater to a diverse population. Hardware stores, dry cleaners, and repair shops serve homeowners. Surf shops and bikini boutiques attract the beach crowd. And Irish pubs, casual cafes, and dance bars bring in evening throngs of young singles, eager to party and meet potential dates.

Manhattan Beach has earned quite a reputation as one of L.A.'s hotspots for the single lifestyle. Locals refer to the area between Pancho's, Brennan's, and Orville and Wilbur's as the "Devil's Triangle"; many singles become "lost" between these three popular dance bars. On many Friday and Saturday evenings, young energetic singles pack these pubs so tightly that long lines wait to get inside.

But the North End business section offers many types of boutiques, cafes, stores, and shops to explore.

1. The Beach Hut

3920 Highland Avenue

When Don Yasui opened this small cafe in 1978, he improvised a breakfast menu which reminded him of the home-cooked meals his Korean family enjoyed in Honolulu. Since then, this inexpensive cafe has become a hit with local surfers, flight stewardesses, and Hawaiian breakfast buffs. The homey decor reflects Don's idea of family dining, as if you were eating in your own cozy Island kitchen. Surf posters and photos clutter the rough walls. But the real treat is not the clientele or funky ambiance but rather the unusual menu, offering Hawaiian sweet bread, spicy Portuguese sausage (made especially for the Beach Hut), fried won ton, scoops of teriyaki-drenched rice, and other Asian-inspired breakfasts. Open daily 7 a.m. to 2:30 p.m.

2. Jo Anne's Chili Bordello

3770 Highland Avenue

Jo Anne, an ex-madam from Jacksonville, Florida, has collected chili recipes from madams across the country, and opened this legitimate "bordello" in 1981. Seventeen varieties of chili, each named after its madam chef, are made from hearty ingredients, including beef, pork, chicken, beer, wine, vegetables, and spices. Inside, you'll swear you're in Belle Watling's parlor, with the red flocked wallpaper, red velvet draped curtains, fancy chandeliers, and honky tonk pianist. Of course, the "girls" who wait on you follow the theme, dressed in tight corsets and silk lingerie, busily serving you under the dulled stares of painted nudes.

3. Orville and Wilbur's

401 Rosecrans Avenue

Both a continental restaurant and a singles dance bar, Orville and Wilbur's serve two clienteles. A dark, casual, intimate restaurant with secluded corner tables offers continental

cuisine in a beach atmosphere. Upstairs, a terraced lounge and bar with ocean views offer live entertainment and dancing in the evenings. Perhaps "the most active bar per square foot in the South Bay," lines often form to get into the bar after 9 p.m.

4. Bruce Grant Surfboards

312 Rosecrans Avenue

For over ten years Bruce Grant has made custom surfboards in the back of this small shop. Inside, a plethora of surfing paraphernalia awaits you, including custom T-shirts, wetsuits, swim fins, surfboard wax, surfing magazines, sunglasses, and stock surfboards.

5. Frank's Bar and Grill

3610 Highland Avenue

Frank Nam, owner of the Hibachi at 120 Manhattan Beach Boulevard (see South Manhattan Beach walk, #32), opened this popular bar and grill in 1977. Most of the menu is similar to the Hibachi's, with daily specials.

6. Pancho's Restaurant

3615 Highland Avenue

Since 1924 an eatery of some kind has existed at this spot. In 1977 Ab Lawrence, the successful owner of Brennan's, rebuilt this two-level Mexican restaurant, decorating it with terraces, lush plants, skylights, and antique treasures. The plush lounge, with its 1895 solid mahogany bar from Emporia, Kansas, serves potent, frosty margaritas. Live bands and singers perform nightly, attracting smartly dressed young singles. But the dining deserves foremost mention. Called "the only gourmet Mexican restaurant in L.A." by *Los*

Angeles Magazine, Pancho's specializes in Mexican seafood dishes. Everything is crisp and fresh, as the kitchen staff, most of whom are from Guadalajara, present sumptuous, authentic Mexican cuisine.

7. Brennan's
3600 Highland Avenue

An Irish-style beach pub with live music, dancing, and dart boards. Although the pub serves only domestic American beer, it makes ''onehelluva'' Irish coffee.

8. Sloopy's Beach Cafe
3416 Highland Avenue

This delightful cafe is a popular hangout for the beach crowd and local hamburger lovers. An open air patio, with barrel and wagon wheel tables, provides plenty of sun and fresh air. Potted flowers, succulents, and cacti mix with the weathered wood sidings to create a rustic ''Beach Calico'' setting for slurping frosty milk shakes, nibbling garden salads, and munching thick sandwiches. Shakes are made in a cornucopia of flavors, including cantaloupe, raspberry, banana, strawberry, peppermint, and mocha.

9. Ron's Nonnos Cafe
3414 Highland Avenue

A comfortable, quaint neighborhood cafe with fresh flowers on the booth tables and counter, Ron's serves traditional American breakfasts. Sample ''Joe's Special,'' a concoction of spinach, onions, eggs, and hamburger, topped with parmesan cheese and served with a fresh banana muffin.

DUNE SECTION

East of Highland Avenue the sand dunes rise further, finally forming a ridge at Grandview Avenue. As George Peck promoted the area in the early 1900's, most homes were first built near the beach. This upper dune area remained underdeveloped until the late 1920's, after Highland Avenue sprouted small businesses.

While the upper dunes remained barren, many Hollywood film studios shot desert scenes on the sandy slopes. One might imagine Rudolf Valentino as the Sheik riding his horse over the dunes.

Today, this neighborhood is experiencing an architectural revitalization with the rest of Manhattan Beach. Many older residences are being remodeled, and a few new homes are being built, including the masterfully crafted neo-Victorian townhouses at Twenty-ninth Street and Alma Avenue.

10. House
3500 Alma Avenue

This two-story modern hacienda, with its walled garden, balconies, and adobe tiles, is noteworthy for its desert landscaping. Large barrel cactus, Mexican fan palms, yucca plants, royal palms, birds-of-paradise, and other sub-tropical flora suggest Bahia de Manzanillo, not the South Bay.

11. Sand Dunes Park
bounded by Grandview and Bell Avenues, Twenty-seventh and Thirty-third Streets

Grandview Avenue follows the dune ridge, its eastern edge

bordering the steep sand dunes as they drop sharply into the narrow valley. From this vantage point, there is indeed a grand view of the inland hills and basin. To the northeast rise the towers of the Chevron oil refinery in El Segundo, resembling an industrial Emerald City with its labyrinth of domed towers and bursts of flame. To the east is the Tree Section, with rows and clusters of tall eucalyptus trees. Immediately down the steep dunes is Sand Dunes Park. Imaginative local residents in the early 1970's constructed stairpaths of railroad ties down the dunes to the park below. In 1983 the city funded redevelopment of the dune pathways and park, creating a unique open area which celebrates the natural terrain. Follow Grandview Avenue to Thirtieth Street. Select a pathway and meander down the dunes, pausing to enjoy the views and flora. Walk through the park to Twenty-ninth Street and from there to Blanche Road.

GASLIGHT SECTION
bounded by Valley Drive, Grandview Avenue, Twenty-first and Twenty-fifth Streets

Once this neighborhood of post–World War II stucco tract houses melted into the monotony of suburbia. But in the late 1970's local residents proposed a unique plan to create a distinctive character for their village. The city worked with the residents and these nostalgic gaslights were positioned along the narrow streets, prompting neighbors to feel a sense of identity and pride in their community.

Today, many of the tract homes have been imaginatively remodeled into cottages and retreats. Front porches, patios, and lush landscaping have followed, encouraging the residents to walk and socialize. Although the gaslights are simple devices, they have contributed much to the neighborhood's revitalization.

12. **Grandview Palms**
Grandview Avenue between Twenty-first and Twenty-third Streets
The stout Canary Island date palms provide ample shade and repose along Grandview Avenue.
13. **Live Oak Park**
bounded by Valley Drive, Seventeenth and Twenty-first Streets
This urban park, nestled between the Sand and Tree sections, is a well-planned and equipped public recreation area, with facilities for baseball, tennis, basketball, and other activities. Walk between the tennis courts and the baseball field. Behind the baseball backstop, climb the stairs up the hill crest to Nineteenth Street. Turn left on Highland Avenue and then walk down Eighteenth Street to the Strand.

SAND SECTION
This northern Sand Section in Manhattan Beach faces the same problems and obstacles as the southern dune area. The steep, unstable slopes and the small lots challenge the townspeople to develop a unique style of residential architecture, utilizing terraces, support walls, hardy ground cover, and densely packed housing.

To maximize enjoyment of ocean views and breezes, nearly every house features balconies, decks, verandas, porches, or picture windows. Most of the narrow streets leading down the sand hill are walking lanes. And as the Sand Section has become more desirable and popular, many houses have been beautifully renovated. As you walk in this neighborhood, enjoy the diversity of architectural styles and designs, each one seemingly celebrating life at the beach, as well as the idiosyncracies of its owner.

14. Eighteenth Street

between Highland Avenue and The Strand
Zigzagging down the steep hill, Eighteenth Street reminds one of a miniature Lombard Street in San Francisco. Note the eclectic mix of houses facing the twisting pathway, as well as the variety of landscaping.

15. Villa Oceana (ca. 1952)

2004 The Strand
This three-story oceanfront house displays a bewildering mix of styles, suggesting a French Riviera villa with American Colonial and Cape Cod detailing. But the statue plant holders and Cambodian stone fresco defy description.

16. House (ca. 1980)

2012 The Strand
A contemporary three-story residence suggesting a modern

Winding downhill to The Strand, Eighteenth Street is a quiet residential footpath bordered by lush landscaping.

hacienda with its thick stucco walls, succulent garden, and glass-enclosed balconies.

17. Townhouses (1983)

2404–B Manhattan Avenue

Manhattan Beach's colony of San Francisco–inspired architecture is further enriched with these twin neo-Victorian townhouses, each with bay windows, antique lamps, and decorative molding.

18. House and Succulent Garden

2420 The Strand

This Pueblo Revival house, with its rounded stucco walls, terraced levels, extended beams, and adobe tile, reinforces its image further with its succulent and cacti garden, edged by a peasant stick fence.

19. Black-Roloff House (1938)

2508 The Strand

Designed by architect Milton J. Black in 1938, this Streamlined Moderne beach residence is accented with porthole windows, steel railings, and glass blocks. The curved smoked glass windows were added to the round observation room by Donald M. Mills, who remodeled the house in 1982.

20. County of Los Angeles Department of Beaches and Harbors (1975)

2600 block of The Strand

This modern structure houses one of the administrative headquarters for Life Guard Services in Los Angeles County.

The Strand, once a sandy Indian footpath, today is a popular pedestrian course following the entire shoreline of Manhattan Beach and affording sweeping views of Santa Monica Bay.

Covering seventy-three miles of county coastline and Catalina Island, Los Angeles County beaches are visited by an average of 75 million people each year. During the summer season, over 1,200 employees staff the Department of Beaches and Harbors, providing for public safety and earning a worldwide reputation as the "finest professional life guards."

21. Duncan House (1981)

2820 The Strand

This imposing modern residence, designed by architect Mark Appell, combines the stark flatness of high-tech exterior design with the softness of beach lifestyle in its interior. Outside, terraced walls rise at odd angles, opening onto

balconies and guaranteeing privacy with smoked glass windows. Inside, a casual yet elegant interior is enhanced with an atrium, a hot tub, a sauna, and stained glass windows.

22. House
3100 The Strand
With its walled garden, sweeping balcony, and semi-tropical landscaping, this Spanish Colonial Revival house reminds one of a villa in Puerto Vallarta.

23. House (ca. 1935)
3421 Manhattan Avenue
A two-story, reinforced concrete house, mixing Zigzag Moderne and Pueblo Revival styling with its sunburst designs above the windows.

EL PORTO

This small developed area, bounded by Rosecrans Avenue, The Strand, Forty-fifth Street, and Highland Avenue, was unincorporated county land until 1981, when its residents voted to join the city of Manhattan Beach. Many people have lived in El Porto for decades and continue to view their community as a distinct village. But the narrow streets, crowded with small houses and duplexes, seem indistinguishable from the rest of the Sand Section.

24. Howe House (1980)
3916 The Strand
Described by its owners as "Western Victorian," this modern yet stylized house might best be labeled "neo-Craftsman," with its rambling quilted brickwork, uneven hand-fashioned beams, and corner tower. Local carpenter Steve Long hand carved the interior and exterior beams, and local craftspersons also produced the brickwork and stained glass windows.

For Further Reading on Manhattan Beach:

Sarah Kerr, "History of Manhattan Beach" (monograph), 1949

The Manhattan Beach Historical Society has also published a number of booklets:

City of Manhattan Historical Committee, "The Streets of Manhattan Beach," 1977

Francis Dow, "Manhattan Beach Yesterdays," 1976

Ellen M. Gleason, "The Manhattan Beach Fire Department: 1923–1973," 1973

Judson Grenier, "A Capsule History of Manhattan Beach: 1912–1976," 1976

Linda Chilton McCallister, "The Waterfront of Manhattan Beach," 1978

Mary Pyatt and Janet Schulpke, "The Neptunian Club of Manhattan Beach: 1909–1974," 1974

PALOS VERDES ESTATES WALKS

Palos Verdes Peninsula is an idyllic setting of terraced hills, rugged canyons, and rocky sea cliffs south of the Los Angeles Basin. Jutting into the ocean between Santa Monica Bay and San Pedro Bay, the Peninsula's Mediterranean climate and landscape have inspired numerous Italian villas, French Riviera retreats, and Spanish Colonial Revival estates to be built. Among its villages, Palos Verdes Estates most beautifully reflects this architectural theme in its residential and commercial buildings as well as in its landscaping.

The town's unusual geography reflects the physiography of the whole peninsula. Once the isolated hilly region was an island, much like Catalina Island. But gradually over hundreds of millenia, the sedimentary run-off from the northern San Gabriel Mountains created a broad alluvial plain, the Los Angeles Basin, connecting the peninsula to the mainland.

Palos Verdes Peninsula is famous for its thirteen major marine terraces formed by the sedimentary deposits. As the peninsula experienced both uplift and sea-cut erosion, these terraces emerged, creating a stepped landscape. The highest terraces are marked by the greatest amount of erosion, while the lowest are most clearly seen in the sea cliffs and beaches. And along the cliff-edged coastline, numerous coves and rocky points reveal the erosive effect of the sea and winter storms.

These rugged hills and isolated coves were once inhabited by Gabrieleno Indians. Archaeologists and historians have identified ten village sites on the peninsula, including one on the northwestern bluff overlooking Malaga Cove. Excellent boat builders and fishermen, the Indians fished in the bay and regularly paddled their canoes out to the Channel Islands, trading with island villages for steatite. Also known as soapstone, this soft stone was used to make cooking utensils and pipes. Often as the boats returned late at night, villages lit signal fires to guide the fishermen home.

After the Spanish explored the region and established missions, large parcels of land were granted to settlers. In

1784, Governor Pedro Fages provisionally awarded Rancho San Pedro to Juan Jose Dominguez, an aging soldier who had accompanied the Portola expedition in 1769. Covering 75,000 acres, the rancho was the first private land concession in Southern California. Dominguez grazed herds of cattle and horses on the land, which included all of the Palos Verdes Peninsula.

By the 1850's the rugged coast began to attract another type of rancher. Large ocean herds of whales passed along the California coast, attracting enterprising whalers from New England. Several whaling stations were established in sheltered coves on the Palos Verdes Peninsula, including Portuguese Bend and Malaga Cove. For years these whaling stations operated, until the great herds of migrating whales were nearly depleted.

For forty years the peninsula continued to be largely uninhabited and unused. In 1894, Harry Phillips, a mining engineer and excellent land manager, was hired by a real estate developer to supervise the peninsula's development. Phillips increased the herds of cattle, and at Portuguese Bend he leased land to enterprising Japanese farmers and their families. Along the northern slopes, barley fields were planted for grain and hay. And in Malaga Canyon, Phillips planted hundreds of eucalyptus trees.

In 1921, E. G. Lewis, an experienced and successful real estate promoter, formed a partnership with Frank A. Vanderlip. Despite initial financial and promotional difficulties, Lewis and Vanderlip formed a new company which bought 3,200 acres of property on the northwest corner of Palos Verdes Peninsula. A select group of city planners and landscape architects was recruited to design the new community, including Frederick Law Olmsted, Jr., Charles H. Cheney, and Myron Hunt.

A better team of planners could not have been selected. Olmsted excelled as a landscape architect, reflecting the invigorating imagination of his father, who designed many notable projects, including Central Park. Cheney had been praised as one of the nation's finest city planners, as evidenced in his work in Fresno, Palo Alto, Alameda, Berkeley, and San Rafael. And Hunt had achieved a reputation as an outstanding architect for his residential designs throughout Southern California.

Palos Verdes Estates, Inc. immediately established restrictions on development to protect the land's beauty and to ensure a picturesque, countrified community. One-half of the acreage was designated as parklands and public rights of way. Ninety percent of the available lots were allotted for carefully designed single family residences. Roads were built to preserve the natural topography.

Under strict design limitations, four communities were planned — Malaga Cove, Lunada Bay, Miraleste, and Valmonte. Each community was to be built around a central plaza edged by arcaded commercial buildings. All structures were to be styled after Mediterranean, country English, or

French Normandy architecture. Exacting regulations concerning architectural and landscape designs highlighted the master plan for the new towns.

To supervise the towns' growth and development, two civic organizations were formed. The Art Jury oversaw the designs of all residences and plantings, enforcing the detailed planning restrictions. The second organization, the Palos Verdes Home Association, assumed civic government responsibilities.

A vigorous real estate promotion began. La Venta, a romantic hilltop inn, welcomed prospective buyers to its idyllic Mediterranean setting. By 1925, one hundred thousand trees and shrubs had been carefully placed throughout the terraced hillsides and shadowy canyons. Soon the first homes began to be built.

Malaga Cove attracted the most intense development. By 1930 a public library, a central arcaded plaza, numerous villas, an ornate school, and a community swimming pool had been built among its hills and canyons.

The Depression, however, caused serious problems for the young town. Although the planners had drawn up a master plan for the entire peninsula, only a small percentage of the lots had been sold, primarily in Malaga Cove. Property owners were unable to keep up parkland maintenance fees, and soon the Palos Verdes Homes Association was behind in its county taxes. The ambitious development not only slowed in sales, but the county threatened to take possession of the unincorporated town's parklands.

In 1939, amid heated debate, the residents of Palos Verdes Estates voted by a narrow margin to incorporate as a city. The Homes Association then collected delinquent property assessments from both Palos Verdes Estates, Inc. and individual owners, thus paying back taxes and securing city control over the parklands.

But the peninsula's original master plan was never revived. Although other developments were built on the peninsula, only Palos Verdes Estates mirrored the designs of the original planners. And of the city's four principal communities, only Malaga Cove built an ornate central plaza as envisioned by the founders. Nevertheless, the Art Jury and Homes Association continued to follow the restrictive guidelines on residential architecture throughout the city.

Today, Malaga Cove stands apart as the community which most fully reflects the imaginative, romantic designs of the original planners. This chapter presents three walks, each of which explores a particular area of Malaga Cove. The first walk leisurely meanders from Malaga Cove Plaza to Malaga Canyon, surveying the town's central plaza, and a wooded residential area amid tall stands of eucalyptus trees. The second walk descends into the lower marine terraces which overlook both Malaga Cove and Bluff Cove. Finally, the third walk explores the middle hillside terraces, enjoying both startling vistas and secluded wooded terraces.

MALAGA COVE PLAZA
AND MALAGA CANYON WALK

1. Malaga Cove Plaza
2. Neptune Fountain
3. Malaga Park Pathway
4. St. Francis Episcopal Church
5. Plaza del Norte
6. Apartments
7. Apartments
8. Via Pinale
9. Farnham Martin's Park
10. Malaga Cove Plaza Library
11. Via Corta

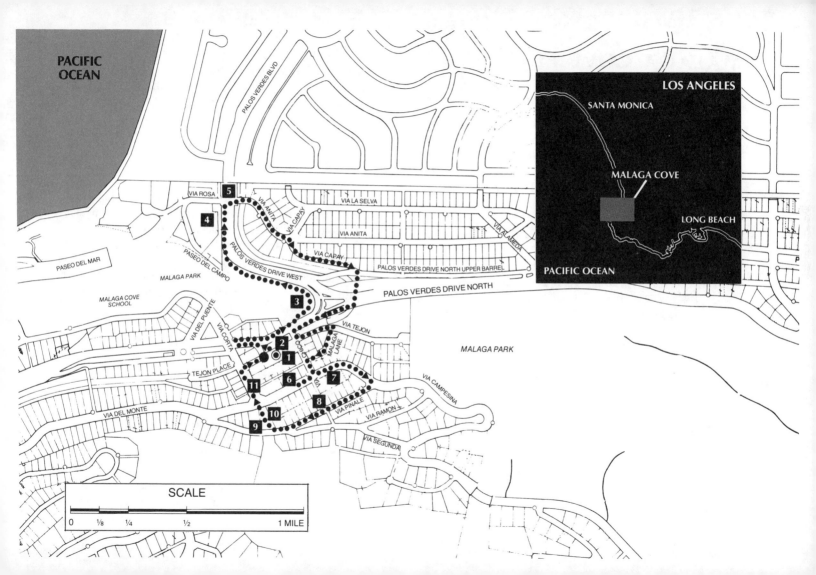

PACIFIC
OCEAN

LOS ANGELES

SANTA MONICA

MALAGA COVE

LONG BEACH

PACIFIC OCEAN

PALOS VERDES BLVD

VIA ROSA

VIA LA SELVA

VIA ANITA

VIA ANITA

VIA CAPAY

VIA CAPAY

VIA ALAMEDA

PALOS VERDES DRIVE NORTH UPPER BARREL

PASEO DEL MAR

PASEO DEL CAMPO

PALOS VERDES DRIVE WEST

MALAGA PARK

MALAGA COVE
SCHOOL

PALOS VERDES DRIVE NORTH

MALAGA PARK

VIA DEL PUENTE

VIA CORTA

VIA TEJON

VIA CHICO

MALAGA LANE

VIA TEJON

VIA CAMPESINA

TEJON PLACE

VIA PINALE

VIA RAMON

VIA DEL MONTE

VIA SEGUNDA

1 2 3 4 5 6 7 8 9 10 11

SCALE

0   1/8   1/4   1/2   1 MILE

MALAGA COVE PLAZA AND MALAGA CANYON WALK

DIRECTIONS: *Take I-405 (San Diego Freeway) and exit south on Crenshaw Boulevard. Follow Crenshaw Boulevard to Palos Verdes Drive North and turn right (west). As this drive meets Palos Verdes Drive West, turn left and follow two blocks to Malaga Plaza.*

PARKING: *Some streets around Malaga Plaza have ample free parking.*

PUBLIC
TRANSPORTATION: *RTD lines 225, 226, 443.*
DISTANCE: *About one and a half miles.*
DURATION: *A leisurely two hours, including breakfast.*
SUGGESTED
ITINERARY: *Begin with coffee, juice, and danish at the Sidewalk Cafe and Bakery, 57 Malaga Cove Plaza (in the rear patio of the Gardner Building).*

1. Malaga Cove Plaza (1924–30)

Palos Verdes Drive West between Via Chico and Via Corta

When the town's original master plan was completed, each of its four principal communities was to be built around a central plaza lined with arcaded commercial structures. Malaga Cove Plaza, with its colonnaded rows of Spanish Colonial Revival buildings, was the only plaza built after these original concepts. Designed by Webber, Staunton, and Spaulding in 1924, the buildings are accented with patterned brick, striking towers, and intricate grillwork. The Gardner Building (57–58 El Tejon) was the first commercial structure built in Palos Verdes Estates; its dedication in 1925 marked a significant moment in the town's growth.

2. Neptune Fountain

Courtyard of Malaga Cove Plaza

Donated by the Palos Verdes Project to the community in 1930, this marble statue is a two-thirds scale replica of the famous bronze "La Fontana del Nettuno" in Bologna, Italy. The original Neptune, erected in 1563, was carved by Gian Bologna and the ornate pedestal by Palermita Lauretti. This reproduction once graced the courtyard of an old Italian villa north of Venice. Today, the fountain and the Plaza create a serene setting of old world charm and elegance.

3. Malaga Park Pathway

paralleling Palos Verdes Drive West between Via Chico and Via Rosa

This narrow asphalt pathway follows Palos Verdes Drive West and leads to St. Francis Episcopal Church and Plaza del Norte. Lined with eucalyptus trees and shrubs, the path attracts many walkers and joggers, who enjoy the views of lower Malaga Canyon and the ocean.

4. St. Francis Episcopal Church

Via Rosita below Palos Verdes Drive West

The pointed roof of the modern church structure rises above the surrounding eucalyptus grove and creates a landmark in

Malaga Canyon. Walk down the brick pathway and steps to the older brick chapel and the stark church courtyard, enjoying the quiet serenity.

5. Plaza del Norte (1924)

Palos Verdes Drive West at Via Rosa

Begun in 1924 as one of the Olmsted brothers' first Peninsula landscaping projects, this northern entrance into Palos Verdes Estates was planted with hundreds of flowering trees and shrubs. Prospective buyers entering the town site immediately passed through a gateway of lush, Elysian gardens, framed by the terraced hills and deep canyons.

6. Apartments (1937)

2433 Via Campesino

Surrounding a central courtyard and reflecting pool, these apartments suggest an ancient Roman villa, complete with textured stone walkways and statues. Large ornate planters, iron gates, and a tiled conical tower add to the picturesque setting.

7. Apartments (1939)

2508–2512 Via Campesino

This four-story terraced apartment structure, designed after the International Style, stands apart from the Spanish-style complexes surrounding it.

8. Via Pinale

between Via Campesino and the Library

Shaded by California pepper trees and sycamores, this quiet

In the courtyard of Malaga Cove Plaza, the ornate Neptune fountain is surrounded by Spanish Colonial Revival arcades.

narrow road is lined with a number of understated Spanish Colonial Revival houses, several of which were built before 1930 (Numbers 2523, 2509, 2325, and 2324). Note the low-pitched roofs covered with terra cotta tiles, the walled gardens, and the balconies laced with iron grilles.

9. Farnham Martin's Park

opposite 2332 Via Pinale

Surrounding a circular lawn, tall pines and elms shade this peaceful park. Its steep hillside is terraced with stone retaining walls, steps, and shrubbery. At the lower end a graceful fountain splashes from a stone pedestal buttressed by sculpted dolphins. Palos Verdes flagstone covers the plaza. The park was named for Farnham B. Martin, former superintendent of parks of the Palos Verdes Project, who was killed in an auto accident in 1928. Martin designed much of Malaga Cove's plantings and supervised their installation and maintenance.

Patterned brick, intricate grillwork, and arched colonnades accentuate Malaga Cove Plaza's walkways.

10. Malaga Cove Plaza Library (1926–28)

2400 Via Campesino

Originally the library for all of the Palos Verdes Peninsula, this seven-level Spanish Colonial Revival structure was designed by Myron Hunt and H. C. Chambers. Inside, a collection of 35,000 books is enhanced by beamed ceilings, antique furniture, and sweeping views. The Olmsted brothers developed the landscaping.

11. Via Corta

between Via Campesino and Tejon Place

Overreaching Moreton Bay fig trees shade this short block, nearly hiding a diverse collection of brick Spanish-style buildings. Note the various towers, arches, balconies, and doorways behind the tree branches and hedges.

Suggesting a Roman villa, this festive apartment courtyard at 2508 Via Campesina is adorned with statues, patterned stone walks, and fountains.

MALAGA HILLS WALK

1. Monterey Style House
2. Italian Villa
3. Houses and Flagstone
4. Comstock House
5. Schoolcraft House
6. Somonte Canyon Path
7. Via Arriba
8. Pathway
9. Pathway
10. La Rive Gauche

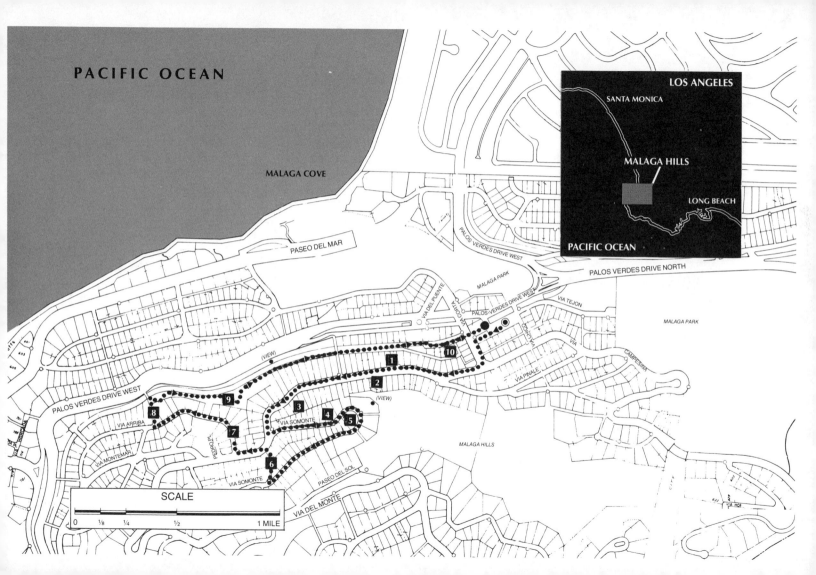

PACIFIC OCEAN

MALAGA COVE

PASEO DEL MAR

LOS ANGELES

SANTA MONICA

MALAGA HILLS

LONG BEACH

PACIFIC OCEAN

PALOS VERDES DRIVE NORTH

MALAGA PARK

PALOS VERDES DRIVE WEST

VIA DEL PUENTE

VIA CORTA

MALAGA PARK

VIA TEJON

VIA CAMPESINA

VIA PINALE

VIA

(VIEW)

1

2

(VIEW)

3

4

5

VIA SOMONTE

9

PALOS VERDES DRIVE WEST

8

VIA ARRIBA

7

PEDRO PL.

6

MALAGA HILLS

VIA MONTEMAR

VIA SOMONTE

PASEO DEL SOL

10

SCALE

0   1/8   1/4   1/2   1 MILE

VIA DEL MONTE

MALAGA HILLS WALK

DIRECTIONS: *Take I-405 (San Diego Freeway) and exit south on Crenshaw Boulevard. Follow Crenshaw Boulevard to Palos Verdes Drive North and turn right (west). As this drive meets Palos Verdes Drive West, turn left and follow two blocks to Malaga Plaza.*

PARKING: *Some streets around Malaga Plaza have ample free parking.*

PUBLIC
TRANSPORTATION: *RTD lines 225, 226, 443.*

DISTANCE: *Less than two miles, but with steep uphill lanes, stairpaths, and gravel roads.*

DURATION: *Allow three hours with tea, rests, and views.*

SUGGESTED
ITINERARY: *Begin with afternoon tea with scones at the Sidewalk Cafe and Bakery, 57 Malaga Cove Plaza. March or April are the loveliest months to walk, as the hills are verdant and dappled with wildflowers. End the walk with wine and cheese at La Rive Gauche.*

VIA DEL MONTE
between Via Corta and Via Somonte

Via del Monte, the major road from Malaga Cove Plaza to the upper hill terraces, is lined with Italian villas and Spanish houses. Large picture windows, balconies, and decks accent most residences as they capture the panoramic views of Malaga Cove and Santa Monica Bay. Extensive plantings create an arboretum of Mediterranean flora. Among the more notable houses are:

1. **House**
   557 Via del Monte
   A Monterey Style house, suggesting early California with its adobe walls, extensive balconies, and palms.
2. **House**
   564 Via del Monte
   An ostentatious modern Italian villa, with stone lions and balustrades.
3. **Houses**
   636–648 Via del Monte
   Extensive use of Palos Verdes flagstone characterizes these homes, in their retaining walls, steps, and facing.

From this secluded public path in the wooded Malaga Hills, a breathtaking view of the South Bay appears through pines and eucalyptus.

VIA SOMONTE
between Via del Monte and Somonte Canyon

Precariously twisting up the steep hillside, this narrow lane affords breath-taking views. As you walk uphill, pause to view the Spanish-style homes as well as the panoramas. Two older residences are particularly noteworthy:

4. Comstock House (1927)
763 Via Somonte
This house clings to the hillside with its three levels of brick walls and balconies.

5. Schoolcraft House (1927)
749 Via Somonte
Commanding sweeping views from its precarious perch, this two-story Spanish-style house features thick flagstone retaining walls, French doors, shuttered windows, and a circular corner sunroom.

From the roadside of 752 Via Somonte, stop to survey the spectacular view of Malaga Cove and the South Bay below. Malaga Cove Plaza, hemmed by towers and arcades, is surrounded by the textured terra cotta roofs of Mediterranean buildings. North Malaga Canyon appears as a dense forest of dark green eucalyptus. The coastline leads from the steep sea cliffs above Malaga Cove northward to the wide sand beaches of Redondo, Hermosa, and Manhattan. Modern high-rises, their metallic skins shimmering in the sun, rise inland behind the coastal hills, and the round towers of refineries dot the horizon. On clear days the distant white towers of downtown Santa Monica float above the bay as Malibu curves to the west. Sailboats cluster near the entrances to Marina del Rey and King Harbor in Redondo Beach. With such magnificent views of the entire Santa Monica Bay, one understands how people can brave the steep hillsides and dare to build such cliff-hanging residences.

6. Somonte Canyon Path
opposite 820 Via Somonte
Walk down this shady, obscure pathway. Formed of flagstone steps and an earthen trail, the path winds its way down Somonte Canyon to Via del Monte. Spiny Canary Island date palms and dense orange pittosporum overshadow the trail. Over twenty miles of public rights-of-way interlace the city's hillsides, but only a few are as well designed and planted as this pathway.

7. Via Arriba
between Via del Monte and Via Lazu
Edging the hillside, this quiet road also provides dramatic views of Santa Monica Bay. Number 1801, a modern Spanish-style ranch house, is fronted by a unusual mix of succulents and cacti.

8. Pathway
opposite 1700 Via Arriva
Follow the crosswalk into the footpath, which is hedged by dense foliage. Descend about fifty yards until the rugged trail meets a dirt road as it switchbacks up the hillside. Walk up the road, which quickly levels out into a wide pathway through a wooded hillside.

9. Pathway

parallelling Palos Verdes Drive North

This public pathway, which provides immediate access to city water mains buried in the hillside, also allows urban hikers and joggers to enjoy a secluded route in a wooded setting. Stands of pines and eucalyptus embrace the hillsides as nasturtium, anise, mustard, and ivy hug the rocky soil. Occasionally peacocks strut along the trail or screech from treetops. Magnificent vistas of Malaga Cove and Santa Monica Bay again appear, this time through silhouettes of towering trees. As the road bends into Somonte Canyon, young coastal redwoods grow near the cool stream bed. A closer look at the arroyo creek reveals layers of flat flagstone, bared by winter rains. As the hillside begins to level into a terrace, rows of fruit trees and flower gardens edge the back road. Follow the wide pathway until it meets the paved cul-de-sac of Tejon Place.

10. La Rive Gauche

320 El Tejon

An elegant yet cozy restaurant serving traditional French cuisine, La Rive Gauche offers a moderately priced, varied menu and an exceptional wine list. Inside, a long country French dining room complete with a fireplace, lace curtains, brass fixtures, and linen provides a quaint setting for dining. On weekends a harpist performs, adding to the romantic ambiance. Diners may also sip wine al fresco on the patio. The menu specializes in fresh fish and poultry, including pheasant and squab. Winner of numerous awards for its excellent wine list, La Rive Gauche offers over 1200 domestic and European wines. Sunday brunch is served from 11:00 a.m. to 3:00 p.m., and reservations are recommended for evenings.

MALAGA COVE AND BLUFF COVE WALK

1. Memorial Park
2. Malaga Path Parkway
3. Malaga Cove Pathway
4. Olmsted House
5. Roessler Memorial Pool
6. Neighborhood Church
7. Moore House
8. Via Media
9. Contemporary Houses
10. Shoreline Preserve
    Pathway
11. "Douglas Cut"
12. Via Almar
13. Malaga Cove School
14. Via Arroyo Pathway

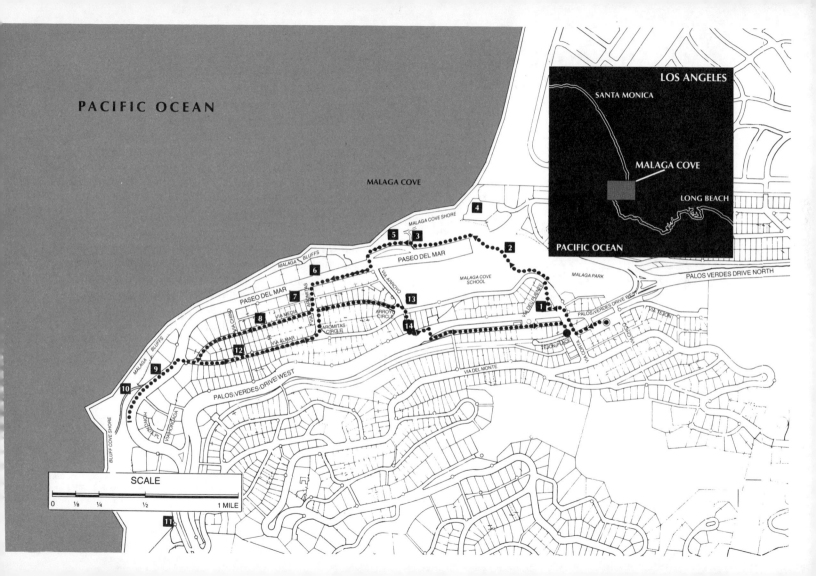

MALAGA COVE AND BLUFF COVE WALK

DIRECTIONS: *Take I-405 (San Diego Freeway) and exit south on Crenshaw Boulevard. Follow Crenshaw Boulevard to Palos Verdes Drive North and turn right (west). As this drive meets Palos Verdes Drive West, turn left and follow two blocks to Malaga Plaza.*

PARKING: *Some streets around Malaga Plaza have ample free parking.*

PUBLIC TRANSPORTATION: *RTD lines 225, 226, 443.*

DISTANCE: *About two miles of gently sloping hills and terraces.*

DURATION: *Approximately two hours with rests and views, excluding dinner.*

SUGGESTED ITINERARY: *Begin an hour and a half before sunset at Malaga Cove Plaza. Conclude your walk with a quiet dinner at La Rive Gauche, 320 El Tejon. (You may want to make reservations before your walk.)*

1. **Memorial Park** (1924)

Via Corta and Palos Verdes Drive West
Planted with eucalyptus trees and shrubs, this triangular park is dedicated to three Palos Verdes Estates residents who lost their lives in World War II.

2. **Malaga Park Pathway**

between Via Corta and Paseo del Mar
As Via Corta bends in its descent into the lower terrace, this well-used pathway branches towards the softball field and Malaga Cove. Walk along the trail. To the right, Malaga Canyon twists toward the sea, its furrowed rim dense with chaparral. Follow the path across the field to the gazebo which overlooks Malaga Cove.

3. **Malaga Cove Pathway**

below the gazebo
From the vantage point of the gazebo, you can survey another path which descends into Malaga Canyon to Malaga Cove Shores. During the summers the path is a popular route for local families and young surfers as they walk to the sandy beach below the steep sea cliff. In fact, this shore is the only sandy beach on the peninsula. Locals call it ''Rat Beach,'' meaning ''Right After Torrance.''

4. **Olmsted House** (1924)

2101 Rosita Place
The large Spanish Colonial Revival estate which sits at the edge of the bluff across the canyon was the permanent home of Frederick Law Olmsted, Jr. In the 1933 Long Beach

A 1925 view of Malaga Cove reveals the windswept hills and barren cliffs before extensive building and planting. Only a few structures have been built, including the Olmsted House (foreground), the Malaga Cove School (with its crowned tower), and La Venta Inn (atop the hill). Courtesy of the Palos Verdes Public Library.

earthquake, a section of the cliff-edged terrace collapsed into Malaga Cove.

5. **Roessler Memorial Pool** (1930)

Paseo del Mar at Via Arroyo

This reinforced concrete pool and clubhouse were originally called the ''Palos Verdes Swimming Club.'' Later named after Fred Roessler, for twenty-five years the mayor of the city, the pool is a popular summer recreation center.

6. **Neighborhood Church** (1928)

415 Paseo del Mar

Originally the residence of J. J. Haggerty, this stately Italian villa was designed by architect Armand Monaco. Extending 290 feet along the ocean bluff overlooking Malaga Cove, the grand residence was anchored with a four-story observation tower. Twenty rooms, originally decorated with antique furnishings and Italian Renaissance frescos by mural painter A. E. Disi, include arched coffers and beamed ceilings. The siting and landscaping were designed by the Olmsted brothers. Haggerty also built a pier into Malaga Cove to launch his boats; rumors, however, speculated that he smuggled antiques and artwork by night. In 1960, the Neighborhood Church bought the estate for $65,000.

7. **Moore House** (1956)

504 Paseo del Mar

Designed by architect Lloyd Wright in 1956, this futuristic house features extensive eaves which fan out above terraced levels.

8. **Via Media**

between Via Aromitas and Paseo del Mar

Walk up Via Aromitas and note the gnarled, contorted carob trees, bent by the force of ocean winds. Turn right on Via Media, a peaceful street lined with elm trees and typical Spanish-style houses.

9. **Houses**

601–609 Paseo del Mar

Situated at the edge of the Malaga Cove bluffs, these contemporary estates bespeak the wealth of newcomers to the city. Massive and grandiloquent, Number 609 resembles a French chateau on the coast of Gironde.

10. **Palos Verdes Estates Shoreline Preserve Pathway**

left of 609 Paseo del Mar

In 1969, the California Coastal Commission and Palos Verdes Estates established this shoreline preserve, which runs the entire length of the city's coastline. Over 130 acres of city-owned bluff and shore parklands are included in the preserve. Further residential development has been prohibited along the bluff so that open fields of wild grass, scenic overlooks, and numerous footpaths remain in public domain. This wide, partially paved path descends into Bluff Cove, passing Flat Rock Point immediately below. Many other paths, however, are gravelly, steep, and dangerous. On the rocky shore beneath the rugged cliffs, tidepools and solitude await the beachcomber. Skin and scuba divers frequent Bluff Cove's shallow waters.

11. "Douglas Cut"

Palos Verdes Drive West above Bluff Cove

In October 1923, sixty tons of blasting powder were set off 320 feet above Bluff Cove and moved 300,000 cubic yards of earth, creating the "Douglas Cut." The cliffside cut allowed Palos Verdes Drive to connect San Pedro and Redondo Beach in a level route, thereby avoiding the old stage road which slowly and dangerously descended into Bluff Cove and then ascended the steep climb to Malaga Canyon.

12. Via Almar

between Paseo del Mar and Via Arroyo

Return to Malaga Cove along this narrow street. Picturesque villas and Spanish-style houses peer from the sloping hillside into Santa Monica Bay.

13. Malaga Cove School (1926)

300 Block of Via Almar

Designed by architects Allison and Allison, this Spanish-style school is dominated by an ornate octagonal tower with a pointed crown.

14. Via Arroyo Pathway

between Via Almar and Palos Verdes Drive West

Walk up this pathway bordered by musty oleander bushes. Carefully cross Palos Verdes Drive West and follow the asphalt road above and paralleling the Drive back to Malaga Cove Plaza.

For Further Reading on Palos Verdes Estates:

Augusta Fink, *Time and the Terraced Land,* 1966
Mary Eva Thacker, "A History of Los Palos Verdes Rancho, 1542–1923," 1923

SAN PEDRO WALKS

One of Los Angeles' oldest settlements and the world's largest manmade harbor, San Pedro offers exciting places for urban walking. Situated on the eastern slopes of the Palos Verdes Peninsula twenty-three miles south of downtown L.A., the community of San Pedro overlooks the ocean and the harbor. In its old downtown, Greek and Yugoslavian restaurants stand next to Italian delis and Mexican cinemas, revealing San Pedro's diverse ethnic communities. In the bluff-edged neighborhood south of downtown, rows of weathered Victorian houses line quiet streets, portraying San Pedro's history. Along the harbor's docks and channels, oil tankers, luxury liners, fishing boats, and yachts are anchored, reflecting the area's sea-oriented economy.

Today, the San Pedro Harbor is known officially as the Port of Los Angeles. Its channels are dredged to fifty-one feet and lined with the most modern shipping facilities and cargo handling systems, creating over 7,000 acres of land and water and twenty-eight miles of waterfront. Yet two hundred years ago the harbor was nothing but mudflats, sand bars, and a huge tidal estuary averaging two feet in depth. Numerous rocky islands dotted the wetlands, which were edged on the west by sea cliffs and bluffs.

The first European to anchor in San Pedro Bay was Juan Rodriguez Cabrillo in 1542. Grass fires started by Indians either to signal fishing canoes or flush out small game, filled the sky with smoke when Cabrillo first saw the region. He called the bay ''Bahia de los Fumos y Fuegos'' (the Bay of Fire and Smoke). Cabrillo left without going ashore.

The next Spaniard to enter the bay was Sebastian Vizcaino. Commissioned by the Spanish viceroy in Mexico to explore and chart the California coast, Vizcaino anchored his ships in San Pedro Bay on November 29, 1602. Landing near present-day Fort MacArthur, Vizcaino named the site in honor of St. Peter, thus establishing the second oldest named community in California after San Diego.

Jose Dolores Sepulveda settled in San Pedro in 1804. By 1835 the Sepulvedas had built several adobe houses and a crude landing in San Pedro. Although most of the peninsula remained barren and uninhabited, the shallow harbor was attracting many ships seeking to trade otter furs for hides and tallow from the inland missions and ranchos. Because of the sandspits and shallow water, ships anchored a mile or so off shore and sent cargo and passengers to shore in small boats called lighters. Because the harbor was distant from local authorities and presidios, smuggling was common.

Richard Henry Dana, who arrived in San Pedro in 1835, described the harbor in *Two Years Before the Mast:*

> I also learned, to my surprise, that the desolate-looking place we were in furnished more hides than any other port on the coast. It was the only port for a distance of eighty miles, and about thirty miles in the interior was a fine plane country, filled with herds of cattle, in the center of which was the Pueblo de Los Angeles—the largest town in California—and several of the wealthiest missions: to all of which San Pedro was the seaport.

A primitive adobe house, built by American ship agents in 1822, provided storage for hides and lodging for sailors on the bluff near Sepulveda's Landing. Cargo had to be pushed uphill or brought down the steep bluff.

Between 1823 and 1850, San Pedro Bay was the busiest port on the California coast; only after statehood and the Gold Rush did San Francisco become the major port. But the Gold Rush also increased the demand for hides and tallow from ranchos around Los Angeles. During this time San Pedro Bay attracted a few enterprising developers who recognized the harbor's potential.

In 1852, August Timms bought the wharf and storehouse which had been built and operated by the Sepulveda family. Timms acquired the rocky point and shorelands surrounding the dock as well, renamed Timms' Landing. He built his residence, a bathhouse, and warehouses at the site.

He was joined by a number of other American entrepreneurs, including a young man from Delaware named Phineas Banning. An aggressive and insightful businessman, Banning owned a wharf, a stageline, and several barges. In 1857, he began a real estate partnership which bought 2,400 acres of Rancho San Pedro four miles northeast of Timms' Landing in the back estuary. He envisioned a new city and harbor at the site which would someday become a major Pacific seaport.

But the problems of shallow waters, mudflats, and slow overland transport faced Banning. He responded by proposing to dredge a main harbor channel and to construct a railroad between Los Angeles and the new town (called New San Pedro and later changed to Wilmington after Banning's hometown). Mud scows dredged a channel into the inner harbor and hand pumps removed water from marshlands. Wharves, warehouses, and lumberyards were soon joined by a fleet of shallow-draft lighters and steamships. The new town was protected from Santana winds and storms by a huge sandspit called Rattlesnake Island.

In 1868, Banning began the Los Angeles and San

Pedro Railroad and secured public bonds for construction. One year later Southern California's first railroad was in operation. In 1871, Congress appropriated monies for the construction of a breakwater at the mouth of the harbor between Rattlesnake Island and a rocky promontory called Deadman's Island. This jetty redirected currents and dredged a deeper channel in the harbor. Los Angeles was on its way to becoming a major seaport.

In 1881, the Southern Pacific developed San Pedro further by extending a railway on deep-pile trestles over tidelands to Timms' Point. Now both trains and freight could reach deep water. That same year San Pedro was incorporated and began a rivalry with Wilmington's maritime business. San Pedro grew vigorously as ship and freight lines attracted settlers to the town. In fact, all of Los Angeles underwent tremendous growth; in 1883 alone, over 13,000,000 feet of lumber was unloaded at San Pedro's wharves.

Congress, recognizing the potential growth of Los Angeles County, appointed a board of engineers to survey the region's coast to determine the best site for a deep water port. Collis P. Huntington, president of Southern Pacific, had constructed a deep water port northwest of Santa Monica in 1891, and for the next six years he blocked various reports which recommended San Pedro as the best site for the region's deep water port. But finally in 1897, federal monies were directed towards the construction of a nine-mile-long breakwater in San Pedro Harbor. The first rocks were dumped by barge in 1899, and by 1912 the first section was completed, with Angel's Gate welcoming ships through its 2,100 foot wide entrance.

Wanting to acquire port facilities directly under its control, in 1906 Los Angeles annexed a sixteen-mile long and half-mile wide stretch of land. This "Shoestring Strip" extended the city limits south to the edge of the harbor. In 1909, after legal and political disputes, Los Angeles annexed the cities of Wilmington and San Pedro, thus securing the harbor area as its official port. With the completion of the Panama Canal in 1914, the Port of Los Angeles gained further importance. Los Angeles continued to grow tremendously in the 1910's and '20's; the Port of Los Angeles surpassed San Francisco in 1923 as the Pacific Coast's busiest port.

During the early 1900's, another major maritime industry evolved in San Pedro. Along the California coast rich fields of albacore, bonito, anchovy, mackerel, and abalone abounded. As early as 1870, fishermen were attracted to San Pedro as the base for their fishing boats. Seafaring immigrants from around the world settled in San Pedro; Italian, Greek, Portuguese, Yugoslavian, and Japanese communities soon settled around the harbor. Major canneries were built as the commercial fishing industry grew. By 1929, the Port of Los Angeles had become the center for the world's largest fishing industry. Today, more than 200 boats serve 5,000 cannery workers and fishermen from Fish Harbor on Terminal Island.

San Pedro continued to grow as the Pacific Coast's major maritime center. In the 1930's and '40's, shipyards employed thousands of longshoremen, dockworkers, and shipbuilders. Wharves and storage areas were enlarged and modernized. During WWII, military operations built new shipyards to serve the wartime economy. After the war, the petroleum industry developed newer and larger pumping, refining, and storage facilities around the harbor to serve the growing demand for automobile products.

With supertankers and containerships in the 1960's, new demands were placed upon the harbor. Channels were deepened and widened to handle the larger ships. Improved cargo handling systems and shipping techniques produced huge cargo berths and storage terminals. Dredging continued to accommodate the new fleets of superships. Today, the Port of Los Angeles is the world's busiest and largest manmade harbor, serving the entire Los Angeles region.

These two walks in San Pedro explore both the old neighborhoods of the maritime city and the busy commercial harbor area. The first walk begins in the old downtown area of San Pedro and leads to the community's oldest residential neighborhood. From there the tour leads along the harbor, exploring fish markets, tourist shops, maritime museums, and passenger terminals.

The second walk surveys the southern section of San Pedro. Exploring Point Fermin, the tour leads to the Upper Reservation of Fort MacArthur. Zigzagging downhill to Cabrillo Beach and the outer harbor, the walk returns to Point Fermin. Both walks will guide you into sites and settings which reflect the colorful history of San Pedro Bay.

OLD SAN PEDRO WALK
AND HARBORFRONT WALK

1. San Pedro City Hall
2. Monument to "Bloody Thursday"
3. Ferry Building and Maritime Museum
4. Port of Los Angeles Administrative Offices
5. Papadakis Taverna
6. Warner Brothers Theater
7. Portofino Italian and Yugoslavian Market
8. Hobby Nobby Restaurant
9. Allstate Bank
10. Cozy Corner
11. Ante's Restaurant
12. Episcopal Seamen's Center
13. Norwegian Seamen's Church
14. Post-modern House
15. Federal Customs House and Post Office
16. Victorian House
17. Neo-Georgian House
18. Danish Castle
19. Rutherford House
20. Selleck House
21. Victorian House
22. Peck House
23. Smith House
24. Spanish-style Houses
25. Misagal House
26. Yugoslav Auditorium
27. Timms' Landing
28. Canetti's Seafood Grotto
29. Municipal Fish Market
30. Fishing Slip
31. Ports O'Call Village

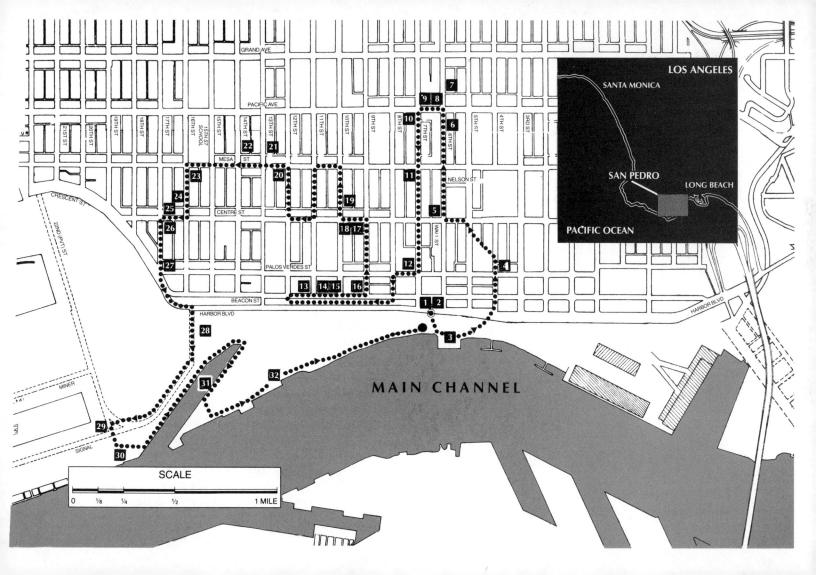

OLD SAN PEDRO WALK AND HARBORFRONT WALK

DIRECTIONS: *Take I-110 (Harbor Freeway) south and exit Harbor Boulevard (immediately before Vincent Thomas Bridge). Continue on Harbor Boulevard to Seventh Street and turn right. Beacon Street is one block down.*

PARKING: *In the neighborhood south of downtown along Eighth and Ninth Streets, ample parking exists.*

PUBLIC TRANSPORTATION   *RTD lines 146, 147, 446.*

DISTANCE: *About two miles of easy walking.*

DURATION: *Allow four hours to stroll, browse, eat, and relax.*

SUGGESTED ITINERARY: *Begin early on a weekday morning from the San Pedro City Hall, at the corner of Beacon Street and Seventh Street. On the walk, stop for breakfast at the Hobby Nobby, Billie's, or the Cozy Corner. End the walk with a late lunch at Ports O'Call Village.*

CLOTHES: *Inconspicuously working class: blue jeans, flannel shirt, and tennis shoes.*

DOWNTOWN SAN PEDRO
bounded by Harbor Boulevard, Pacific Avenue, Fifth and Seventh Streets

When August Timms bought Sepulveda's Landing in 1852, only a few small fishing shanties occupied this little valley. Over the next thirty years, as Banning's new Wilmington port attracted most of the maritime trade, a small lumbering community called Fayal grew here.

In 1881, however, San Pedro entered a new era. Southern Pacific built a deep-pile railroad trestle over the tidelands from Wilmington to San Pedro, thus bringing both freight and passengers directly to deep water. The new railway ended near Timms' Point, not far from this draw. Additional tracks were laid, along with terminals, warehouses, wharves, and docks. By 1884 San Pedro's growing maritime operations forced Wilmington's port to close. The new harbor's commercial center grew; soon its wooden stores and boardwalks bustled with shipping agents, dock workers, passengers, and new settlers.

In the early 1900's, as the federally funded breakwater created the world's largest manmade harbor, the fishing and canning industries of San Pedro established themselves as the nation's largest. Many immigrants from seafaring countries around the world settled here. Downtown and the harborfront were vibrant with cafes, hotels, and businesses catering to Italians, Greeks, Yugoslavs, Portuguese, and Japanese.

However, by the 1950's downtown had changed from a bustling seaport to a depressed tenderloin district. Its old brick buildings harbored cheap cafes, rundown hotels, dancehalls, and seedy taverns. While many long-timers valued the district as historic and colorful, others saw it as unsavory and blighted.

The city responded by adopting the Beacon Street Redevelopment Plan in 1968. In order to effectively realize this commercial district, eleven square blocks comprising more than two hundred structures, some nearly a century old, were leveled. Streets were reconstructed to handle more traffic, and vacant lots were left as gaping reminders of urban renewal's ultimate solution. One can only wonder how much history and character was lost to this simplistic solution.

Today, a few blocks remain as empty lots. Others are partially developed with unimaginative cinder block buildings. Fortunately, however, several blocks of the old commercial district escaped destruction. Turn-of-the-century brick storefronts, Beaux Arts banks, Art Deco offices, and a few Victorians remind the city walker of what architectural delights must have been lost.

As you walk in this older section, note the various detailing, moldings, signs, and fronts which accent the structures. Wander in many of the thrift stores, specialty shops, cafes, and bookshops which give the area a feeling of a small town.

1. San Pedro City Hall (1928)
corner of Beacon and Seventh Streets
A stately seven-story civic center, this building houses departments and services of local government, as well as the San Pedro Bay Historical Society.

2. Monument to "Bloody Thursday"
corner of Beacon and Sixth Streets
On May 15, 1934, a group of union members involved in San Pedro's first major maritime strike broke into Berth 145 and disrupted the living quarters of non-union workers. Police and private guards fired rifles and tear gas, killing two protestors and seriously wounding five. Called "Bloody Thursday," this incident led to a settlement which improved union members' wages, working conditions, and living standards.

3. Ferry Building and Maritime Museum (1940)
foot of Sixth Street
The Municipal Ferry Building operated from 1940 to 1963 on Berth 84, its Streamlined Moderne ramps and gates crowded with thousands of passengers and workers traveling between San Pedro and Terminal Island. In 1963, when the 6,050-foot-long Vincent Thomas Bridge opened, the ferries stopped. Today, the building hosts the Los Angeles Maritime Museum, the only institution which focuses exclusively upon Southern California's nautical heritage. Its ship models, paintings, documents, and historical photographs trace San Pedro Bay's growth from Indian canoes to supertankers. The Museum is listed as Los Angeles Historic Cultural Landmark Number 146.

4. Port of Los Angeles Administrative Offices (1981)
425 South Palos Verdes Street
This five-story contemporary office building, designed by architect John Carl Warnecke, headquarters the administrative

offices of the Port of Los Angeles. This building suggests a ship's superstructure in drydock, with the massive exposed steel girders, wire cabled balconies, and heavy concrete foundation. The inside lobby is sleek and modern with fountains, glass blocks, and high-tech lighting.

5. **Papadakis Taverna**

   301 West Sixth Street

   This family-run moderately priced restaurant offers traditional and regional Greek cuisine, including superb souvlaki, garithes glifatha, and moussaka. On occasion, waiters add to the lively setting by dancing.

6. **Warner Brothers Theater** (1931)

   478 West Sixth Street

   Architect B. Marcus Priteca designed this splendid Zigzag Moderne cinema in 1931. Its reinforced concrete structure is decorated with florid reliefs and geometric banded surfaces.

7. **Portofino Italian and Yugoslavian Market**

   530 West Sixth Street

   Owner Joseph Pizzocchieri offers outstanding selections of both Italian and Yugoslavian specialty items, including prosciutto, cotta, baccala, campari, torrone, and baci. Walk inside and examine the shelves of pasta, dried and salted fish, fresh baked breads, imported wines and beers.

8. **Hobby Nobby Restaurant**

   615 South Pacific Avenue

   A landmark coffee shop in San Pedro where many local folk regularly meet. Although the menu is conventional and predictable, its meals are quick, inexpensive, and satisfying. Sit at the corner in Miss Vicki's section; she has worked here for eighteen years.

9. **Allstate Bank** (ca. 1925)

   643 South Pacific Avenue

   Assyrian lion figures and designs are etched in the columned walls of this classic bank, reflecting the stylistic revivals of the 1920's which also produced Egyptian housecourts, Babylonian tire factories, and Mayan hotels in Los Angeles.

10. **Cozy Corner**

    299 West Seventh Street

    And yet another funky local cafe! Stepping inside transports you into a 1951 Coca-Cola ad, with the formica counter, red vinyl stools, old Coke machine, cheap breakfasts and chatty owner. Open weekdays.

11. **Ante's Restaurant**

    729 South Palos Verdes Street

    Walk inside this cheery, comfortable Yugoslavian restaurant featuring Dalmatian specialties. Owner Ante Perkov offers dishes ranging from fresh seafood to cevapcici, raznjici, mostaccioli, and sarma.

BEACON STREET AND SAN PEDRO PLAZA PARK
Beacon Street between Eighth and Eleventh Streets

Extending along the bluff's edge, Beacon Street overlooks the harbor and offers panoramic views. During the past century, many structures have been built along Beacon Street, from Victorian and Post-modern residences to Spanish Colonial Revival and Streamlined Moderne commercial structures. In the 1960's the park was relandscaped with pathways, benches, and gazebos. This section of Beacon

Street reminds one of Santa Monica's Ocean Avenue and Palisades Park, but on a smaller scale.

Walk along the park's sidewalk to Eleventh Street, enjoying the harbor view. Walk back to Ninth and enjoy the diverse architecture along Beacon Street, including the following:

12. Episcopal Seamen's Center
101 West Eleventh Street
A meeting hall and social gathering place for both active and retired seamen. The small Episcopal chapel is quaint and serene.

13. Norwegian Seamen's Church (1951)
northwest corner of Beacon and Eleventh Streets
Sponsored and staffed by the Norwegian Lutheran Church, this center provides Scandinavian seamen a home away from home. Its meeting hall, chapel, reading lounge, kitchen, cantina, and recreational facilities serve both the social and spiritual needs of the Nordic community around the harbor.

14. House (1981)
1017 Beacon Street
A bold, stark Post-modern residence, sharply contrasting with neighboring Craftsman Style houses, with its corrugated steel facing, plywood walls, and exposed steel girders.

15. Federal Customs House and Post Office (1935)
Beacon Street at Ninth Street
An imposing yet graceful P.W.A. Moderne Post Office, its interior richly detailed with Deco accessories and a captivating forty-foot mural by Fletcher Martin.

OLD SAN PEDRO
bounded by Beacon Street, Pacific Avenue, Eighth and Seventeenth Streets

The first home in this bluff-top area, the oldest residential neighborhood in San Pedro, was built by August Timms near Beacon and Fifteenth Streets. Only a few permanent settlers followed Timms, until 1881, when Southern Pacific built this railway to San Pedro's waterfront. As the commercial district grew, newcomers settled on this mesa. Many houses built balconies, verandas, porches, and even a few widow's walks to capture views of the harbor entrance, the busy wharves, and the passing ships.

When Old San Pedro was first platted in the 1880's, the earliest homes were Italianate and Victorian. Over the past century many Craftsman and Spanish-style houses have been built as well. As the population became less well-to-do, many of the larger homes were subdivided into apartments.

Today, the district is a quiet, lower middle class neighborhood. Mom-and-pop groceries dot the blocks. Although many houses are weathered and in disrepair, the architecture attests to the settlement's early history. Numerous Victorian and early Craftsman Style houses, bordered by white picket fences and shade trees, line the streets. Several outstanding houses are listed below, but the neighborhood offers such a rich array of old residences that one hopes to see the area designated a historic district, as it clearly reflects the life of Old San Pedro.

16. **House** (ca. 1889)

918–920 Centre Street

A late Queen Anne Victorian featuring a large cupola and ornate scrollwork.

17. **House** (ca. 1905)

936 Centre Street

Huge wooden columns support the front of this two-story Georgian Colonial manor.

18. **Danish Castle** (ca. 1885)

324 West Tenth Street

Constructed by a Danish sea captain, this Queen Anne house surveys the harbor from its third-story spindled balcony and corner tower.

19. **Rutherford House** (1890)

1216 South Mesa Street

A beautifully remodeled two-story Victorian house with twin front bay windows and rows of gables.

20. **Selleck House** (ca. 1918)

428 Thirteenth Street

A magnificent Craftsman Style house, with oversailing roofs supported by variegated wooden beams which are Oriental in character.

21. **House** (ca. 1891)

424 Fourteenth Street

Another delicately remodeled Victorian house with intricate gingerbread trim.

This late Queen Anne Victorian house at 918 Center Street testifies to the rich architectural heritage of old San Pedro.

22. Peck House (ca. 1885)

382 Fifteenth Street

This Eastlake Victorian house, with its paneled surfaces, shingles, exposed posts, and dentils, was built by George Peck, who platted much of this neighborhood in the late 1880's. Interestingly, Peck also subdivided and developed much of Manhattan Beach in the early 1900's. Moved to this site in 1915 from Beacon and Fourteenth, the house is sadly in disrepair.

23. Smith House (ca. 1886)

337 Sixteenth Street

Built by a New England sea captain, this clapboard house is one of the oldest residences in San Pedro. Early residents decorated the short stone wall with abalone shells.

24. Houses (ca. 1925)

1619–1639 Centre Street

Four one-story Spanish-style houses marked with adobe tiles, whitewashed stucco walls, and garden patios.

25. Misagal House (ca. 1895)

262 Seventeenth Street

Another Victorian residence, whose widow's walk and spindlework balcony once overlooked Deadman's Island and the harbor entrance.

26. Yugoslav Auditorium (1935)

corner of Beacon and Seventeenth Streets

A bland, reinforced concrete Moderne meeting hall which serves the Yugoslavian community.

PORT OF LOS ANGELES HARBORFRONT

Encompassing nearly 7,000 acres of wharves, basins, terminals, and channels, the Port of Los Angeles includes twenty-eight miles of waterfront. Each year thousands of commercial vessels pass through Angel's Gate, bringing 100,000 tons of cargo each day. With the most modern cargo handling and transport systems, the port is a kaleidoscope of maritime activity.

While much of the harborfront bustles exclusively with cargo facilities, a few stretches are designed for pedestrians. This section of the walk meanders along these waterfront paths, surveying fishing docks and browsing in picturesque Ports O'Call Village, a complex of shops and restaurants along the harbor's main channel.

27. Timms' Landing

foot of Fifteenth Street near the South Pacific slip

From the crumbling concrete bridge of Signal Street, you see below a section of railroad tracks overgrown with tumbleweeds and wild mustard. The first Port of Los Angeles was developed at this site by Diego Sepulveda in 1824. August Timms bought the sandy point in 1852 and improved its facilities to handle the Gold Rush demand for local beef, hides, and tallow. He enlarged the point by towing the hulls of shipwrecks, which collected sand deposits, to the site. By 1860 Timms had built his residence, storehouses, wharves, and a small hotel, all served by his stagecoach line to Los

Angeles. In 1871 a jetty was constructed from Timms Landing south about 600 feet. Southern Pacific built a new railroad terminal here in 1881. But in 1907, as planners designed the new harbor, dredging, filling, and leveling made Timms Point and Landing unrecognizable. The site is registered as California State Historical Landmark Number 384.

28. Canetti's Seafood Grotto
309 East Twenty-second Street
This spacious, warehouse-like restaurant specializes in seafood, selected fresh each morning across the street at the Municipal Fish Market.

29. Municipal Fish Market
Berth 72 at the foot of East Twenty-second Street
An expansive structure measuring 80 by 420 feet, this market provides cleaning, processing, storage, and office facilities to fish wholesalers. Trucks line the ramps in the early mornings as 3,000 retailers are supplied from the market.

30. Fishing Slip
between Sampson Way and the Fisherman's Dock
Walk along the perimeter of this slip, lined with dozens of fishing boats. Many of these boats fish in local waters for bonita, snapper, and mackerel. When they return to dock, their nets must be cleaned and repaired. As you walk, you will see piles of nets along the wharf, as well as gulls and pelicans.

31. Ports O'Call Village
between Berths 74 and 83
Stroll through this narrow waterfront commercial development. Its picturesque paths lead to many delightful specialty shops and quaint restaurants. Although the theme of fishing villages suggests just another Southern California tourist park, Ports O'Call is really quite charming. The architecture changes from Old Boston's North End to Monterey's Cannery Row. Many of the restaurants offer harborfront dining, where you can relax and observe the maritime activities on the main channel. A number of harbor tours are available from Ports O'Call, as well. Wander into the fresh fish markets and, if you're in the mood, pick some live crabs or lobsters, order them steamed, and crack the delicacies in public eating areas along the waterfront.

The bluffs of old San Pedro, lined with old hotels, Victorian houses, and Canary Island date palms, rise above San Pedro Harbor's fishing slip.

POINT FERMIN WALK

1. Pacific Diner
2. Ayre's Castle
3. Gaffey Summit Viewsite
4. Fort MacArthur Upper Reservation
5. Point Fermin Park and Lighthouse
6. Walker's Cafe
7. Blue Anchor Inn
8. Thirty-ninth Street Stairpath
9. Cabrillo Beach Museum

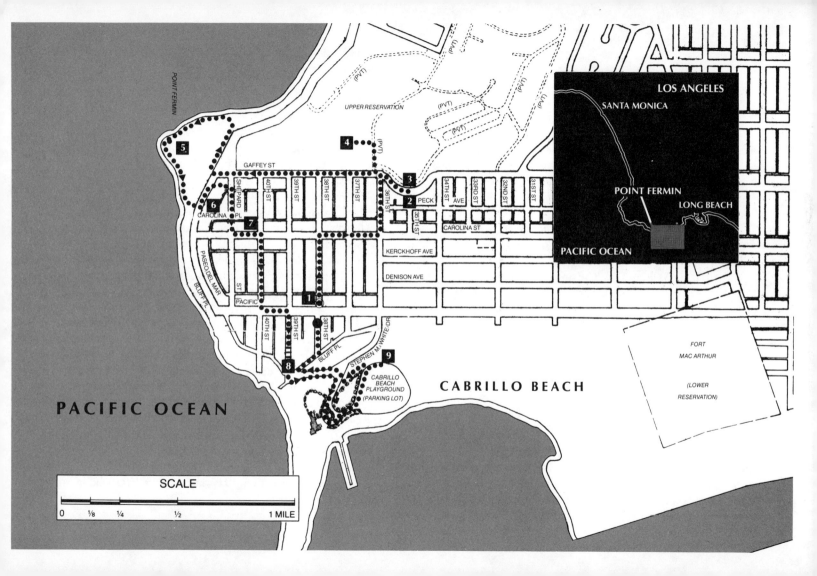

POINT FERMIN

LOS ANGELES

SANTA MONICA

POINT FERMIN

LONG BEACH

PACIFIC OCEAN

UPPER RESERVATION

(PVT)

GAFFEY ST

SHEPARD ST

40TH ST

39TH ST

38TH ST

37TH ST

36TH ST

34TH ST

33RD ST

32ND ST

31ST ST

AVE

35TH ST

CAROLINA ST

KERCKHOFF AVE

DENISON AVE

PECK

CAROLINA PL

PACIFIC

PASEO DEL MAR

BLUFF PL

40TH ST

39TH ST

38TH ST

BLUFF PL

STEPHEN M. WHITE DR

CABRILLO BEACH PLAYGROUND
(PARKING LOT)

CABRILLO BEACH

FORT
MAC ARTHUR

(LOWER
RESERVATION)

PACIFIC OCEAN

SCALE

0   ⅛   ¼   ½   1 MILE

POINT FERMIN WALK

DIRECTIONS: *Take I-110 (Harbor Freeway) south and exit on Gaffey Street. Continue south on Gaffey Street and turn left on Twenty-second Street. After two blocks turn right on Pacific Avenue and drive to Thirty-eighth Street.*

PARKING: *The residential neighborhood west of Pacific Avenue has plenty of parking.*

PUBLIC TRANSPORTATION: *RTD line 446.*

DISTANCE: *Less than two miles with some hilly walking.*

DURATION: *Allow four to six hours, including breakfast, museum browsing, rests, and views.*

SUGGESTED ITINERARY: *Begin with breakfast at the Pacific Diner, 3821 Pacific Avenue (open everyday but Monday).*

Because this area is so compact and homogenous, the walk examines only points of interest rather than neighborhoods. As you explore the Point Fermin area, however, note the predominant Craftsman Style houses with their low roofs, extended eaves, exposed wooden beams, shingled sides, porches, horizontal windows, and occasional stained glass windows.

1. Pacific Diner
3821 Pacific Avenue
A cozy, friendly diner serving scrumptuous breakfasts and lunches. Popular among local residents; long lines often form for Sunday brunch in this rustic cafe. Closed Mondays.

2. Ayre's Castle (1925)
3437 Peck Avenue
Built by Vern Ayre, a stunt aviator and Alaskan bush pilot, this flamboyant residence was supposedly patterned after a Scottish castle. Yet its gooey turrets and melted stucco walls resemble more a sand-castle. Recently the house has been remodeled, refining its stature as it overlooks the harbor.

3. Gaffey Summit Viewsite
Gaffey Street between Thirty-fourth and Thirty-ninth Streets
Walk up the narrow parkway to the summit of Gaffey Street. Below you stretches a panoramic view of the harbor, including the outer breakwater, channels, cranes, ships, Long Beach, refineries, and Vincent Thomas Bridge. On clear days the outline of Catalina Island is etched on the southern horizon.

4. Fort MacArthur Upper Reservation
entrance at Gaffey and Thirty-ninth Streets
Most of this 116-acre tract was purchased in 1910 by the government as the primary site for fixed armament to protect the newly constructed harbor. Three major gun emplacements were built from 1914 to 1917, including underground storage

areas, tunnels, work rooms, concrete control buildings, and fourteen-inch guns. Much of the southern reservation has been reassigned as Angel's Gate Park. As you walk through the Thirty-ninth Street gate, you immediately notice the *Korean Friendship Bell,* a Bicentennial gift to the United States from South Korea. The seventeen-ton cast bronze bell is the largest outside of Asia. From the pagoda and park grounds, you can survey the southern sea cliffs of the Palos Verdes Peninsula.

5. Point Fermin Park and Lighthouse

Gaffey Street at Paseo del Mar

This twenty-eight-acre park of broad lawns, massive Moreton Bay fig trees, towering palms, shaded pergolas, and promenades, is the site of one of California's oldest lighthouses. The point was named by British sea captain George Vancouver in 1793, in honor of the presidente of California's missions, Fermin Francisco de Lasuen. Phineas Banning proposed that a lighthouse should be built here as early as 1858. In 1874 the lighthouse was finally constructed, complete with four-story cupola and Eastlake Victorian detailing.

6. Walker's Cafe

700 Paseo del Mar

Owned by Bessie Walker, who began this cafe with her husband in 1944, Walker's is a lively, funky, kitsch-filled pub catering to local folk. Its bar and dining room feature paintings, statues, and knick-knacks only a Brooklyn

Constructed in 1874 to guide ships past treacherous rocks, the Point Fermin Lighthouse today is a state and city historical landmark.

grandmother would love. But the rowdy, friendly, cheerful clientele create a place where you can guzzle a beer, down a burger, and "shoot the bull" with no pretensions.

7. Blue Anchor Inn (1922)
405 Carolina Street
A Craftsman Style quadplex saluting the harbor with its flagpole in the front yard and a wood-crafted gate picturing an American flag.

8. Thirty-ninth Street Stairpath
Thirty-ninth Street above Bluff Place
At the end of this secluded street, walk down the concrete stairpath to Bluff Place. A sweeping view of the outer harbor and Cabrillo Beach spreads below you.

9. Cabrillo Marine Museum (1982)
3720 Stephen White Drive
Walk down Oliver Vickery Circle to the statue of Juan Rodriguez Cabrillo, who in 1542 was the first European to anchor in San Pedro Bay. Walk north to the Post-modern Cabrillo Marine Museum. Designed by Frank O. Gehry in 1982, the architecture creates an odd, playful image with its use of industrial materials, including galvanized steel panels, bare stucco, and canopies of chain link fencing. Inside the museum are exhibits of marine life displayed in aquaria which highlight the natural habitat of the sealife.

Canopies of chain link fencing suggest a huge industrial net over the courtyard of Cabrillo Marine Museum.

For More Reading on San Pedro:

Richard Henry Dana, *Two Years Before the Mast,* 1845
Robert C. Gillingham, *The Rancho San Pedro,* 1961
Charles Queenan, *The Port of Los Angeles,* 1983
Oliver Vickery, *Harbor Heritage,* 1979
Dr. Lois J. Weinman, *L.A. – Long Beach Harbor Areas Cultural Resource Survey,* 1978

INDEX